CAMBRIDGE
PRE-GED
EXERCISE BOOK
in
Reading

CAMBRIDGE Adult Education
Prentice Hall Regents, Englewood Cliffs, NJ 07632

CAMBRIDGE PRE-GED EXERCISE BOOK in Reading

Editorial supervision: Tim Foote
Production supervision: Janet Johnston
Manufacturing buyer: Art Michalez

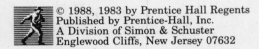 © 1988, 1983 by Prentice Hall Regents
Published by Prentice-Hall, Inc.
A Division of Simon & Schuster
Englewood Cliffs, New Jersey 07632

Printed in the United States of America

10 9 8 7 6 5 4 3 2

ISBN 0-13-114273-9

Prentice-Hall International (UK) Limited, *London*
Prentice-Hall of Australia Pty. Limited, *Sydney*
Prentice-Hall Canada Inc., *Toronto*
Prentice-Hall Hispanoamericana, S.A., *Mexico*
Prentice-Hall of India Private Limited, *New Delhi*
Prentice-Hall of Japan, Inc., *Tokyo*
Simon & Schuster Asia Pte. Ltd., *Singapore*
Editora Prentice-Hall do Brasil, Ltda., *Rio de Janeiro*

CONTENTS

ABOUT THIS BOOK

You can use this book to practice and develop the reading skills that you need for success with the three "reading" tests of the GED. The exercises in this book are divided into five groups, or skill areas:

- Reading for Information—exercises that give you practice at finding main ideas and details in a passage

- Interpreting What You Read—exercises that give you practice in finding unstated main ideas, making inferences based on details in a passage, and drawing conclusions from the information in a passage

- Analyzing What You Read—exercises that give you practice in distinguishing facts from opinions and recognizing an author's attitude toward a subject or intention in writing on a subject

- Reading Tables, Graphs, and Diagrams—exercises that give you practice in getting information from illustrations and making inferences based on that information

- General Review—exercises that help you develop all your reading skills

The charts on the inside covers of this book and of the *Cambridge Pre-GED Program in Reading* show how the lessons in the textbook and the exercises in this book are related.

In each skill area, the exercises are grouped by type of reading material:

general reading   social studies
prose literature   science

The passages in the general reading sections represent the kind of reading you probably do every day—the kind of material with which you always use your reading skills. The prose literature passages were all written by prominent authors. The passages in the social studies and science exercises cover basic concepts in those two areas. When you work through those sections, you will broaden your knowledge of social studies and science as you strengthen your reading skills.

At the end of each section of this book there are Answers and Explanations. You will probably find it useful to check your answers each time you complete an exercise. The explanations will help you understand any questions that you find difficult.

READING FOR INFORMATION

PART A: GENERAL READING

Read each passage. Then choose the correct answer to each question that follows the passage.

TRAIN SCHEDULE TO LAWRENCE

LEAVES			ARRIVES
Hoover	Norton	Ellis Springs	Lawrence
6:15A	6:25	6:32	7:00
7:30A	7:40	7:47	8:15
X 8:05A	——	——	8:35
10:05A	10:15	10:22	10:50
2:05P	2:15	2:22	2:50
X 5:15P	——	——	5:45
6:05P	6:15	6:22	6:50
7:20P	7:30	7:37	8:05
9:30P	9:40	9:47	10:15

A — AM
P — PM
X — Express

1. According to this schedule, when does the 2:05 PM train out of Hoover leave Ellis Springs?

   (1) 2:05   (2) 2:15   (3) 2:22   (4) 2:50

2. According to this schedule, when does the 9:30 PM train out of Hoover leave Norton?

   (1) 9:20   (2) 9:30   (3) 9:40   (4) 9:50

3. According to this schedule, when does the AM express train arrive in Lawrence?

   (1) 8:35   (2) 9:35   (3) 10:35   (4) 2:35

4. According to this schedule, when do express trains leave Hoover for Lawrence?

   (1) 7:30 AM and 6:05 PM   (2) 6:15 AM and 5:15 PM
   (3) 8:05 AM and 6:05 PM   (4) 8:05 AM and 5:15 PM

You do not break boards or bones. There are no grunts or screams. Aikido is a gentle martial art growing in popularity.

Aikido is a Japanese art of self-defense. Aikidoists do not hurt their attackers. They unbalance their attackers and make them fall to the ground. Aikidoists themselves practice falling to escape attack.

Aikido is not only a physical art. It is also an art of the mind. The founder of Aikido said, "The only opponent is within." The attacker is not your enemy. He is only confused about his life. Understand yourself and your attacker. Try to love him.

People study Aikido at a dojo, or school. Teachers are called sensei. Students wear loose, white clothes. Beginners wear white belts. Experts wear black belts. Aikidoists do not compete against one another. Their own improvement brings them closer to a black belt.

Aikidoists use slow, careful movements. They breathe fully with each movement. Arms are often stretched out like swords. Strong arms are not necessary, however. Balance is more important than strength. For this reason, women do as well as men at Aikido.

If you study Aikido, you will play defender some of the time. You will play attacker some of the time. You will be thrown on the mats all of the time. Either way, you'll flip for Aikido.

5. The main purpose of the passage is to describe

    (1) martial arts   (2) self-defense
    (3) Aikido   (4) Japanese culture

6. According to the passage, Aikido is an art of the mind because Aikidoists

    (1) read books about self-defense
    (2) try to frighten their attackers
    (3) use slow, careful movements
    (4) try to understand themselves and their attackers

7. According to the passage, Aikidoists move from a white belt to a black belt by

    (1) competing against each other   (2) improving themselves
    (3) escaping attack   (4) developing strong arms

8. The passage states that all of the following are a part of Aikido EXCEPT

    (1) using slow, careful movement
    (2) breaking boards and bones
    (3) breathing fully with each movement
    (4) stretching arms out like swords

What has no taste, color, or calories and is essential for our diets? Water. We shouldn't take it for granted.

Our bodies are 65 percent water. Our blood is 83 percent water. Maybe we could go 80 days without food. But we could live only 10 days without water.

Water regulates body temperature. It keeps us from getting too hot or too cold. Water also carries off waste from our bodies.

On the average, we need two or three quarts of water each day. Work and hot weather may increase that need. A worker in a desert would need about a gallon and a half of water. People do not get all of their water by drinking. Foods contain water. Apples, for example, are 85 percent water.

When people see a clear glass of water, they think it is pure. It is *not* pure. And, in most cases, it's good that it's not pure. Dissolved minerals in water are important. Water contains calcium, iron, and other minerals. Calcium builds up teeth and bones. Iron is an important part of our blood.

Fluoride is another mineral that is often found in water. Fluoride fights tooth decay. In many places, fluoride is added to drinking water. However, the amount of fluoride that is added has to be carefully watched. Too much fluoride can be harmful.

9. According to the passage, the percent of water in our blood is

   (1) 65%   (2) 80%   (3) 83%   (4) 85%

10. According to the passage, water is needed for all of the following EXCEPT

    (1) regulating body temperature   (2) supplying vitamins
    (3) supplying dissolved minerals   (4) carrying off waste

11. According to the passage, fluoride is added to water to

    (1) help fight tooth decay   (2) build up bones
    (3) build up blood   (4) regulate body temperature

12. Which of the following best states the author's main point?

    (1) Too much fluoride can be harmful.
    (2) People do not get all of their water by drinking.
    (3) Water contains calcium, iron, and other minerals.
    (4) Water is essential for health.

Alzheimer's disease is a major national health problem. Nearly 2 million Americans over the age of 65 have Alzheimer's disease. It is a leading cause of death among the elderly. But Alzheimer's disease is not confined to the aged. There may be a million or more people under the age of 65 suffering from the disease.

At one time, victims of Alzheimer's disease were said to be "getting senile." The disease was thought to be a natural part of growing old. It is now known that Alzheimer's disease strikes young and old alike. It is an organic disease that destroys brain cells.

Alzheimer's disease affects the patient's memory, speech, and movement. In the beginning stages of the disease, the patient may seem slightly confused. He may have trouble speaking. Then the patient's memory begins to fail him. He may forget dates, telephone numbers, names, and places.

As the disease progresses, the patient may not recognize family and friends. These symptoms often cause terrible anxiety in the patient. He may feel lost and frightened. Sometimes the patient reacts with violent and hostile behavior.

In the last stages of the disease, the patient may not be able to take care of himself. He may have lost the ability to speak and walk.

Scientists don't know exactly what causes Alzheimer's disease. It may be caused by a virus. It may be caused by a toxic substance in the environment. At present, there is no cure for the disease. But there are ways to slow its progress. Exercise and physical therapy can help the victims of this disease.

13. The main idea of the passage is that Alzheimer's disease

    (1) is a terrible part of the aging process
    (2) is an organic disease that affects young and old
    (3) can be cured by physical therapy
    (4) causes forgetfulness

14. All of the following are symptoms of Alzheimer's disease EXCEPT

    (1) forgetfulness   (2) difficulty in speaking
    (3) loss of sight   (4) loss of the ability to walk

15. According to the passage, which of the following may be a cause of Alzheimer's disease?

    (1) poisons produced by the brain   (2) getting old
    (3) a virus   (4) lack of exercise

16. According to the passage, the progress of Alzheimer's disease can be slowed by

    (1) surgery   (2) a change in environment
    (3) medicines   (4) physical therapy and exercise

When a person has a drink, the alcohol in the drink is absorbed into his blood. The amount of alcohol in the blood is called the Blood Alcohol Concentration, or BAC.

The BAC depends on several things. They include the amount of alcohol consumed, the amount of time spent drinking, and the person's weight. Using these factors, the National Highway Traffic Safety Administration has worked out a plan to estimate a person's BAC.

The amount of alcohol in a drink varies. But a 12-ounce can of beer has almost the same amount of alcohol as $1\frac{1}{2}$ ounces of 86-proof whiskey. The BAC is estimated by comparing the person's weight to the number of 12-ounce beers or $1\frac{1}{2}$-ounce glasses of whiskey drunk over 2 hours.

A 100-pound person that drinks 4 beers in 2 hours has a BAC of about .10%. However, a 240-pound person that drinks the same amount of beer has a BAC of about only .05%. The person that weighs less has a larger amount of alcohol in his blood.

There are other factors that affect the amount of alcohol in the blood. If a person has eaten before drinking, the alcohol will enter the blood more slowly. Also, studies show that younger people are affected more quickly by alcohol than older people.

17. The best title for this passage would be

    (1) How Alcohol Enters the Blood
    (2) Factors That Affect the Blood Alcohol Concentration
    (3) Whiskey and Beer
    (4) The National Highway Traffic Safety Administration

18. According to the passage, a 12-ounce beer contains about the same amount of alcohol as

    (1) $1\frac{1}{5}$ ounces of 86-proof whiskey
    (2) $1\frac{1}{2}$ ounces of 86-proof whiskey
    (3) .10 ounces of 86-proof whiskey
    (4) .5 ounces of 86-proof whiskey

19. All of the following are used to estimate BAC EXCEPT

    (1) amount of alcohol consumed (2) amount of time spent drinking
    (3) age   (4) weight

20. One man weighs 200 pounds. Another man weighs 100 pounds. Each man drinks two beers in two hours. According to the passage, the man that weighs less will have

    (1) a higher BAC   (2) a lower BAC
    (3) the same BAC   (4) a BAC of .05%

A healthy houseplant can grow to a large size. It can outgrow the pot that you have it in. Repotting a houseplant isn't hard. But it can affect the plant's health, so it should be done carefully.

The first thing you need when you repot a plant is a new pot. It's important to choose the right size pot for your plant. Most plants don't do well if they are moved to a pot that's too large. Choose a pot that's just one size larger than the old pot.

The kind of pot that you choose can also affect your plant's health. A red clay pot with a hole in its bottom works best. The red clay allows the soil to "breathe" easily. The hole provides drainage. It helps to protect the plant from being overwatered. If you use a pot with no drainage, be sure to put about an inch of coarse gravel in the bottom of the pot. This will provide a place for excess water.

After you get the right pot, you need to get the right soil for the plant. Don't use any old dirt. Use potting soil. Potting soil contains nutrients that your plant needs. You can buy pre-mixed potting soil, or you can make your own. Here is a good mixture for most house plants:

> $\frac{1}{2}$ part garden soil
> $\frac{1}{4}$ part peat moss or leaf mulch
> $\frac{1}{4}$ part clean sand
> 1 teaspoon of long-acting fertilizer

Be careful when you repot the plant. Remove the plant from its old pot carefully. The roots of the plant should be disturbed as little as possible. Hold the plant by the stem. Then turn the plant upside down to lift off the old pot. Place the plant on a layer of fresh soil in the pot. Then fill in the pot with more potting soil. (Pack the soil in lightly.) Water the plant, and the job is done.

21. The best title for this passage would be

  (1) Watering Houseplants   (2) Planting a Garden
  (3) Repotting Houseplants   (4) Making Potting Soil

22. According to the passage, a pot with a hole in the bottom

  (1) allows the soil to "breathe" easily   (2) is made of clay
  (3) provides a place for excess soil   (4) provides drainage

23. All of the following are ingredients for potting soil EXCEPT

  (1) peat moss   (2) clay   (3) sand   (4) fertilizer

24. The passage states that after you remove a plant from its old pot, you should

  (1) place the plant on a layer of fresh soil in the new pot
  (2) empty the soil from the old pot into the new pot
  (3) water the plant
  (4) pack the soil in the new pot

Check your answers on page 19.

PART B: SOCIAL STUDIES

Read each passage. Then choose the correct answer to each question that follows the passage.

The United States operates under a federal system of government. Under the federal system, power is divided between the central government and the states. The central government is given specific powers. These powers are named in the Constitution. Powers that are not assigned to the central government in the Constitution belong to the states.

The central government can pass laws that affect trade between states. The central government can also make treaties with foreign countries. It has the power to print money. The Constitution gives the central government these powers. These powers belong to the central government only. However, the states have many powers that the central government can't control. For example, a state is allowed to tax people who live and work in the state. The central government can't put a limit on the amount of money that a state taxes its people.

Most people feel that the federal system has many good points. One good point is that it restrains the power of the central government. The central government cannot become too powerful. Another good point is that the central government makes sure that the bigger states don't become too powerful. Under the Constitution, all states are treated equally. The laws of the central government do not favor one state over another.

1. The main idea of the passage is that power under the federal system is

   (1) divided among the states
   (2) given to the central government
   (3) given to the states
   (4) divided between the states and the central government

2. According to the passage, a good point about the federal system is that

   (1) bigger states have more power than smaller states
   (2) states have the same powers that the central government has
   (3) the central government cannot become too powerful
   (4) the central government can put a limit on state taxes

3. All of the following are powers of the central government EXCEPT

   (1) passing laws affecting trade between the states
   (2) limiting state taxes
   (3) printing money
   (4) making treaties with foreign countries

4. The powers of the central government are assigned to it by

   (1) the state governments   (2) the Constitution
   (3) Congress   (4) the Supreme Court

Two representatives in Congress wanted bills passed last year. Jean Morris, a Democrat, wanted a jobs bill. However, she didn't really want a bill to help farmers get out of debt. Dan Blake, a Republican, wanted a bill to help farmers get out of debt. But he didn't really want to pass another jobs bill. They both lost. And they both won.

Jean Morris represents a coal-mining state. Last year, some big factories in the country closed down. These factories used coal. The coal business suffered. Many miners lost their jobs. Morris wanted to get jobs for these workers. She knew that the jobs could win her votes on Election Day.

Blake had a similar problem. There were many farmers in his state. Many of the farmers owed a lot of money to banks. They had borrowed the money to improve their farms. But there was a surplus of crops. Because farmers had grown too much, crop prices were low. Farmers couldn't make enough money to pay their debts. Some farmers even lost their farms. The people in Blake's state weren't happy. They wanted the government to do something. They wanted a bill that would help the farmers out. Blake supported such a bill. If it passed, the government would buy off the extra crops that the farmers grew.

Morris and Blake got together. Morris promised to vote for the farm bill if Blake would vote for the jobs bill. Blake agreed to do it. This way, they both would have a better chance to pass the bill they really wanted.

Morris and Blake practiced "quid pro quo." "Quid pro quo" means "this for that." It is a trade. Each lawmaker wants to pass a bill. Neither one really likes the other's bill. But they agree to vote for both bills. This way, they both get what they want.

5. The main purpose of this passage is to explain

    (1) the problems of the coal business
    (2) the practice of "quid pro quo"
    (3) why Dan Blake had no interest in a jobs bill
    (4) why some farmers lost their farms

6. According to the passage, there is unemployment in Morris's state because

    (1) miners cannot pay their debts to banks
    (2) miners are losing their homes
    (3) the coal-mining industry is suffering
    (4) coal prices are too low

7. The passage states that Dan Blake wanted to pass a bill that would

    (1) give farmers new jobs
    (2) improve the farmers' land
    (3) pay farmers' debts
    (4) make the government buy farmers' extra crops

8. According to the passage, Blake agreed to vote for the jobs bill because if he voted for it

    (1) Morris would vote for the farm bill
    (2) the farmers would get their land back
    (3) the coal miners would vote for him
    (4) the economy would be stronger

In the United States today, there are two major parties — the Democratic Party and the Republican Party. Each political party is made up of members who share goals and ideas. Each party wants its goals and ideas to direct the actions of government.

Parties nominate, or choose, people that they want in office. The nominated people are called candidates. Political parties select candidates to represent them in elections. Each party then works to get its candidates elected.

The list of candidates that a party nominates is called a slate. The government has elections on national and state levels. There are also smaller elections on county, ward, town, and precinct levels. The party presents voters with a slate that covers each level of government.

Nominating candidates is the major job of a party. But it is not the only thing that a party does. At national conventions, party members from every state gather together. They make up a platform. A platform is a statement of goals. The goals may be general or specific. For example, a general goal may be having better schools. A more specific goal may be raising teachers' salaries. The platform creates unity for the party. It tells voters what the party stands for.

A party must also do fund-raising. Fund-raising is a group of activities designed to bring in money. The party uses some of this money to pay for its day-to-day operation. But most of the money is spent on getting the party's candidates elected.

9. The main idea of the passage is that a political party is organized so that its goals and ideas can

   (1)   bring in money
   (2)   get candidates elected
   (3)   direct the actions of government
   (4)   raise teachers' salaries

10. According to the passage, a platform is

   (1)   a fund-raising event   (2)   a political party
   (3)   a list of candidates   (4)   a statement of goals

11. According to the passage, the major job of a party is to

   (1)   nominate candidates   (2)   raise teachers' salaries
   (3)   make a platform   (4)   do fund-raising

12. According to the passage, each of the following is true about political parties EXCEPT

   (1)   parties nominate candidates for office
   (2)   the two major parties often have the same platform
   (3)   political parties use money from fund-raising to get their candidates elected
   (4)   political parties want their goals and ideas to direct the actions of government

For more than a century, the two major parties in America have been the Democratic and the Republican parties. But from time to time, other parties have been created. A new party is formed when a group of people is not happy with the two major parties. This party is called a "third party."

One example of a third party is the Populist Party. In the 1880's and 1890's, farmers were not satisfied with the two major parties. Farmers were not making much money. They called for an inflation of the currency. This means making more money available to the people. They were also unhappy about the railroads. Railroads charged high prices for shipping their goods. Farmers wanted government to control the railroads. The two major parties did not agree with the farmers.

In 1892, farmers from all over the country met. They formed a third party called the People's Party, or the Populist Party. The members of the party drew up a list of goals. These goals included government ownership of all transportation and communication systems and the inflation of the currency. The party also tried to get support from workers in the cities. It called for an eight-hour work day.

In 1892, the Populist Party ran James Baird Weaver for president. Baird did not win the election. However, he received many votes — more than one million. Many other Populist candidates did win their elections. They were elected governors, senators, and congressmen.

In 1896, the Populist Party did not run a candidate for president. It supported the Democratic candidate, William Jennings Bryan. Gradually, most members left the Populist Party to join the Democratic Party. The Populist Party was not strong enough to survive. But it is an example of how a need for change can result in the creation of a new party.

13. The central idea of the passage is that third parties are formed when

  (1) a group is unhappy with the two major parties
  (2) the two major parties are not strong enough to survive
  (3) people are not making enough money
  (4) unemployment is high

14. According to the passage, the farmers were dissatisfied with the two major parties because the Democrats and Republicans

  (1) wanted the government to own the railroads
  (2) called for an inflation of the currency
  (3) did not agree with the farmers' goals
  (4) charged high prices for shipping goods

15. According to the passage, all of the following were the farmers' goals EXCEPT

  (1) an eight-hour work day
  (2) reduced unemployment
  (3) government control of the communication systems
  (4) inflation of the currency

16. According to the passage, most people left the Populist Party to join

   (1) the Democratic Party   (2) the Republican Party
   (3) the People's Party   (4) another third party

To most people, an institution may be a mental hospital or a university. But to a sociologist, an institution is something different. A sociologist studies the way that groups of people are organized. To a sociologist, a social institution is a set of beliefs, ideas, and rules that holds a group of people together.

A group of people can have many social institutions. Some common social institutions are the family, religions, and governments. Each of these institutions gives its group a set of beliefs, ideas, and rules. Each institution fulfills a particular human need. The family, for example, fulfills a need for love and emotional support.

Each person in a social institution has a role. A role is the pattern of behavior that is expected of a person. Within the family, for example, there are the roles of mother, father, daughter, and son.

Social institutions may change over time. In recent years, for instance, the family has undergone many changes. Divorce is more acceptable than it used to be. Single parents are learning to fill the roles of both mother and father. But even though they change, social institutions last over long periods of time. Individual families may break up. But the institution of the family has survived for hundreds of years.

17. The main idea of the passage is that a "social institution" is a

   (1) mental hospital or a university
   (2) form of government
   (3) set of roles that an individual plays
   (4) set of beliefs, ideas, and rules

18. According to the passage, all of the following are true of social institutions EXCEPT that they

   (1) fulfill a particular human need
   (2) separate people from their groups
   (3) change over time
   (4) last a long period of time

19. According to the passage, which of the following is an example of how the family has changed?

   (1) Fathers are helping mothers to raise children.
   (2) Mothers are working outside the home.
   (3) Divorce is becoming more acceptable.
   (4) People are getting married later in life.

20. Which of the following is the BEST title for the passage?

   (1) Social Institutions   (2) Sociologists
   (3) Changes in the Family   (4) Roles in Society

Minh Pham was born in Vietnam. He left when he was 21 years old. Minh has been in America for almost two years. There is still much he does not understand about America.

Once, Minh was in a supermarket. He saw an old man and an old woman. They wanted a box of cereal. The box was on a high shelf. The man and woman couldn't reach it. Minh saw a stepladder. He got on the ladder and got the box. He handed it to the elderly couple. They thanked him.

"Where are your children?" asked Minh. "Why don't they help you buy food?"

"Our children have their own lives," said the man and woman. "We like to be independent." Minh doesn't think this is right. In his country, children help their parents. Minh gave the elderly couple his phone number. He told them to call him if they needed help. One night they asked Minh to dinner, but they never asked him for help.

One day, Minh was walking with a Vietnamese friend. The two men were going to a movie. Minh wanted to go to a restaurant first. Minh took his friend's hand. He pulled him toward the restaurant. People on the street stared at Minh. In Vietnam, friends often hold hands. Minh found out that people in America are not used to men holding hands.

Minh Pham is going through a process known as resocialization. Socialization is the process in which a person learns to live in a society. Everyone goes through this process. Minh went through it when he lived in Vietnam. But the Vietnamese way of life is much different from the American way of life. When Minh came to America, he had to learn a new way of life. He had to learn how to live in a new society.

Minh has learned a lot about American life in two years. He still has a lot to learn. The process of resocialization can take many years.

21. The main idea of the passage is that socialization is the way in which a person

   (1) learns to live in a society
   (2) travels from one country to another
   (3) learns to act independently
   (4) learns about America

22. The passage states that Minh did not understand why the elderly man and woman were not

   (1) helping their children   (2) shopping with their children
   (3) holding hands   (4) using a stepladder

23. According to the passage, socialization happens to

   (1) only the Vietnamese in America   (2) only Americans
   (3) only older people   (4) everyone

24. According to the passage, people stared at Minh and his friend because Minh and his friend were

   (1) Vietnamese   (2) holding hands
   (3) arguing   (4) not dressed like Americans

Check your answers on page 20.

PART C: SCIENCE

Read each passage. Then choose the correct answer to each question that follows the passage.

Photosynthesis is a very basic process. Without it, life on earth would not exist.

In the process of photosynthesis, green plants do two things. First, they produce glucose. Glucose is a kind of sugar. It is one of the most basic foods on earth. The second thing that green plants do in photosynthesis is to release oxygen into the air. Without the oxygen made by green plants, animal life on earth would not exist.

Only green plants can carry out the process of photosynthesis. That's because green plants contain a substance that no other kind of plant or animal contains. That substance is chlorophyll.

In photosynthesis, a green plant uses three basic ingredients—water, sunlight, and carbon dioxide. Carbon dioxide is a gas that is in the air. The first step in photosynthesis is very simple. Sunlight hits the leaves of the green plant. The chlorophyll in the leaves absorbs the sunlight. The plant uses the sun's energy to change the water that the plant has absorbed. It changes the water by breaking it down into oxygen atoms and hydrogen atoms.

Some of the hydrogen and oxygen atoms recombine to form new water. But some of the hydrogen atoms are used to produce glucose. The plant takes in carbon dioxide through its leaves. It combines the carbon dioxide with the hydrogen atoms to form glucose. Any oxygen atoms that are left over are released by the plant into the air.

1. The main idea of the passage is that photosynthesis is a process by which green plants

    (1) produce glucose and release oxygen
    (2) make chlorophyll and release carbon dioxide
    (3) grow taller and stronger
    (4) turn green and flower

2. The three basic ingredients used in photosynthesis are water, sunlight, and

    (1) oxygen   (2) hydrogen   (3) carbon dioxide   (4) glucose

3. When sunlight hits the leaves of a green plant, the chlorophyll in the plant

    (1) takes in carbon dioxide
    (2) absorbs the sunlight
    (3) changes water into oxygen atoms and hydrogen atoms
    (4) releases oxygen into the air

4. Glucose is formed from

    (1) hydrogen and oxygen atoms
    (2) hydrogen atoms and carbon dioxide
    (3) oxygen atoms and carbon dioxide
    (4) chlorophyll and sunlight

A group of scientists in Florida is trying to do something that hasn't been done before. They are trying to grow a square tomato. They're not using special chemicals or fertilizers. They're using Mother Nature to do it.

The way in which the scientists are trying to grow a square tomato involves a branch of science called genetics. Genetics is the study of heredity. It's the study of how traits get passed on from parents to offspring. A trait is a characteristic that an offspring has. For example, the color of a person's hair or eyes is a trait. It is something that the person has inherited from his parents.

A new tomato plant is like a baby. It inherits the traits of its parents. Normally, tomato plants are self-pollinating. This means that pollen from one tomato plant lands on a pistil of the same plant to produce a new plant. Therefore, a new tomato plant usually has only one parent. It is usually identical to that parent.

Scientists have found that they can cross-pollinate plants to produce new strains of the plant. These new strains, or hybrids, carry the traits of both parent plants. Sometimes, the hybrids carry different traits from their parents. The scientists in Florida are hoping to create a hybrid that yields square tomatoes.

Can the scientists actually come up with a square tomato? Given what they've done in the past, it seems possible. They've already created a hybrid that yields pinkish, low-acid tomatoes. And they've created hybrids that yield harder tomatoes that don't bruise easily.

5. The main idea of the passage is that scientists in Florida are trying to create

    (1) a self-pollinating tomato plant
    (2) a hybrid tomato plant
    (3) a stronger tomato plant
    (4) a low-acid tomato plant

6. The passage states that genetics is the study of

    (1) tomato plants   (2) hybrids
    (3) heredity   (4) pollination

7. According to the passage, scientists can produce new strains of a tomato plant by

    (1) cross-pollinating plants
    (2) allowing plants to pollinate themselves
    (3) treating the plants with special chemicals
    (4) growing the plants in fertilizer

8. According to the passage, a hybrid is

    (1) a tomato plant   (2) a trait
    (3) a self-pollinating plant   (4) a new strain of a plant

Drug and cosmetics companies spend millions of dollars each year to develop new products. They also spend millions of dollars on testing the new products. They test them to make sure that they're safe for humans to use. But the ways in which new products are tested have come under attack from some people.

Each year, drug and cosmetics companies in the U.S. use millions of live animals to test their products. Scientists who work for the companies say that they must use live animals. They claim that the only way to test the safety of a product is to test it on a living animal. On the other hand, some people feel that the tests are cruel to the animals and needlessly painful. They point to two tests in particular — the Draize test and the LD 50 test.

In the Draize test, six live rabbits are used for each test. The substance that is being tested is put into one eye of each rabbit. The other eye is left alone. Scientists look for changes in the eye that was treated with the substance. Any changes in that eye are assumed to be caused by the substance. This test can make the rabbit go blind or die.

The LD 50 test is used to find out how poisonous a substance is. "LD" stands for "Lethal Dose." In this test, increasing doses of the substance are injected into a group of animals until half of the animals die.

Scientists use the information from the Draize test and the LD 50 test to figure out if a product is safe for humans to use. They feel that they can save human lives with the information that they get. They say that the only sure way to test a product is with living animals. Any other kind of test may not give them the information they need.

9. The main idea of this passage is that testing using live animals

    (1) should be stopped
    (2) is necessary to save human lives
    (3) is a widespread practice that is coming under attack
    (4) costs millions of dollars

10. According to the passage, what happens to rabbits in the Draize test?

    (1) They are injected with a toxic substance.
    (2) They have chemicals put in their eyes.
    (3) Their skin is treated with chemicals.
    (4) Blood is taken from them.

11. According to the passage, the purpose of the LD 50 test is to find out

    (1) how poisonous a substance is
    (2) if a substance affects the eyes
    (3) when a substance causes pain
    (4) if a substance harms the skin

12. According to the passage, people who approve of the Draize and LD 50 test feel that these tests

    (1) do not hurt the animals
    (2) are necessary to make sure that products are safe
    (3) can help find a cure for cancer
    (4) should also be performed on humans

During the 50's, 60's, and 70's, a chemical called dioxin began to appear in the environment. Dioxin was a common by-product in the manufacture of many industrial and agricultural products. Small amounts of dioxin remained in some of these products. Larger amounts were found in waste produced when these products were made.

Dioxin may be the most toxic substance ever made by man. Less than 50 millionths of a gram will kill a lab animal within minutes. In even smaller amounts, it has caused cancer and birth defects in animals. The amount of dioxin it takes to kill a human isn't known. But it is known that even the smallest quantity will make a person very ill.

Most of what is known about the effects of this poison on people comes from industrial accidents. Scientists have studied workers who have been exposed to dioxin on the job. They have observed people who have come in contact with waste containing dioxin. Dioxin is much too poisonous to test on humans in a lab.

Dioxin first affects the skin. Contact with dioxin causes painful skin damage that can sometimes leave permanent scars. After the dioxin is removed from the skin, the skin usually heals. But the long-term effects on the body can be much worse.

Dioxin affects many organs within the body. These include the kidneys, spleen and pancreas. But doctors have found that the organ most damaged by dioxin is the liver.

The liver's main function is to clean the blood. It filters poisons out of the blood. Contact with dioxin can cause scar tissue to form on the liver. Scar tissue prevents the blood from moving freely through the liver's filters. Poisons can then build up in the blood.

13. The main idea of the passage is that dioxin

    (1)   is a highly toxic substance
    (2)   causes painful skin damage
    (3)   is used in cruel tests on lab animals
    (4)   is needed to make important industrial and agricultural products

14. The passage states that most information about dioxin's effects on humans comes from research on

    (1)   laboratory subjects   (2)   kidney patients
    (3)   industrial workers   (4)   Vietnam veterans

15. According to the passage, dioxin first affects the

    (1)   liver   (2)   skin   (3)   blood   (4)   kidneys

16. According to the passage, scar tissue on the liver is dangerous because it

    (1)   filters dioxin into the blood
    (2)   prevents the blood from moving freely through the liver
    (3)   can lead to cancer
    (4)   damages the kidney, spleen, and pancreas

"Stress" is a term that is used to describe mental and emotional tensions that people face in life. Doctors have linked stress to such health problems as heart attacks and strokes.

What kind of person is most likely to suffer from a stress-related illness? In the past, doctors believed that high-level business executives were the most likely victims of stress. They felt that executives were more likely to suffer the bad effects of stress because of the pressure of making important decisions. But some studies show that people who work for executives are more likely to suffer from stress-related illnesses than the executives themselves.

Why would workers suffer from stress more than their bosses? Experts point to some reasons. One reason involves the person's outlook on life. A high-level executive is usually a very confident person. This good self-image makes stress easier to deal with. On the other hand, an average worker may not have much self-confidence. He may feel that he can be easily replaced in his job and that his job is not important. A poor self-image can produce stress.

Another reason is the kind of stress that each kind of person has to deal with. For executives, periods of stress usually are very short. Once an executive makes a decision, the period of stress usually ends. Some doctors even say that this kind of short-term stress is good for the body. In contrast, the stress faced by the average worker is usually constant. Worries about job security, money, and the future affect the average worker more than the well-paid executive.

17. The main idea of the passage is that stress-related illnesses occur in

    (1) high-level executives who have to make important decisions
    (2) the average worker more frequently than in the worker's boss
    (3) people who have a poor self-image
    (4) people who have heart attacks and strokes

18. Which of the following is NOT mentioned in the passage as a cause of stress?

    (1) the fear of being fired
    (2) worries about the future
    (3) bad business decisions
    (4) feelings that one's job is not important

19. According to the passage, what do some doctors say about short-term stress?

    (1) It is good for the body.
    (2) It causes health problems in average workers.
    (3) It makes a person lose self-confidence.
    (4) It helps a person make important decisions.

20. According to the passage, which of the following is related to a poor self-image?

    (1) lack of self-confidence   (2) lack of money
    (3) worries about money   (4) worries about important decisions

Acid rain is a very serious air and water pollution problem. Many people feel that it is the most serious pollution problem that we now face. Scientists say that plant and animal life in thousands of lakes in the U.S. and Canada has already been destroyed by acid rain.

Acid rain forms in the upper atmosphere. There, sulfur dioxide and nitrogen oxides mix with water vapor. They mix with water vapor to form sulfuric acid and nitric acid. When the vapor condenses and rain falls, the acids fall with it. Every time acid rain falls in a lake, the level of acid in the lake rises. Over time, it can rise to the point at which plants and insects cannot survive. Without plants, which supply oxygen, and insects, which supply food, fish die. The lake becomes a dead lake.

The problem of acid rain has greatly increased in the last few years. Most of the blame for acid rain has been placed on industries. However, some people feel that ineffective air pollution laws are also to blame for the acid rain problem.

A few years ago, many cities and states passed local air pollution laws. The laws were written to improve the air quality in the cities and states. However, the laws usually didn't say anything about the amount of pollution that an industry could pump into the air. Industries found a way to meet the new pollution laws without reducing the amount of pollution they released. They met the new standards by building taller smokestacks.

With the taller smokestacks, air pollutants were released higher up into the atmosphere. The wind carried them far away from the polluting factory. To the people near the factory, the air seemed cleaner. However, the pollution that they once got was now coming down hundreds of miles away in the form of acid rain.

21. The main idea of this passage is that the problem of acid rain

    (1) is a very serious pollution problem
    (2) will disappear over the next century
    (3) will ruin the fishing industry
    (4) is under control due to government laws and industry cooperation

22. According to the passage, acid rain forms in

    (1) lakes   (2) smokestacks
    (3) the upper atmosphere   (4) plants

23. The passage states that industries reacted to air quality standards by

    (1) disobeying the law
    (2) burying acids in the ground
    (3) reducing the amount of pollution the factories released
    (4) building taller smokestacks

24. According to the passage, acid rain does all of the following in a lake EXCEPT

    (1) poison fish   (2) kill plants
    (3) kill insects   (4) raise the level of acid

Check your answers on page 22.

ANSWERS AND EXPLANATIONS

Part A: General Reading

1. **(3)** The 2:05 PM train out of Hoover leaves Ellis Springs at 2:22 PM. You can find this information in line 5 under Ellis Springs.

2. **(3)** The 9:30 PM train out of Hoover leaves Norton at 9:40 PM. You can find this information in line 9 under Norton.

3. **(1)** The AM express train leaves Hoover at 8:05 AM. The train arrives in Lawrence at 8:35 AM. You can find this information in line 3 under Lawrence.

4. **(4)** There are two express trains that leave Hoover for Lawrence. They are marked by an "X." One train leaves at 8:05 AM and the other train leaves at 5:15 PM.

5. **(3)** The main purpose of the passage is to describe Aikido. Martial arts, self-defense, and Japanese culture may help to describe Aikido, but the passage is mainly about Aikido.

6. **(4)** Aikido is an art of the mind because Aikidoists try to understand themselves and their attackers. You can find this answer in the third paragraph of the passage.

7. **(2)** Aikidoists move from a white belt to a black belt by improving themselves. You can find this answer in the fourth paragraph of the passage.

8. **(2)** Breaking boards and bones is NOT a part of Aikido. Aikido is a gentle art. This is stated in the first paragraph.

9. **(3)** Our blood is 83 percent water. You can find this answer in the second paragraph of the passage.

10. **(2)** The passage does NOT state that water supplies vitamins. The passage tells you that water is needed to regulate body temperature and carry off waste (paragraph 3). The passage also states that water is needed to supply dissolved minerals (paragraph 5).

11. **(1)** Fluoride is added to water to help fight tooth decay. You can find this answer in the sixth paragraph of the passage.

12. **(4)** The author's main point is that water is essential for health. The information in the passage shows why water is essential. The author gives the main point in the first paragraph.

13. **(2)** The main idea of the passage is that Alzheimer's disease is an organic disease that affects young and old. The passage shows that the disease is not confined to old people who are "getting senile." The passage also describes the symptoms, stages, and treatment of this disease.

14. **(3)** Loss of sight is NOT stated as a symptom of Alzheimer's disease. Paragraphs 3, 4, and 5 describe the symptoms of the disease.

15. **(3)** Some scientists think that Alzheimer's disease may be caused by a virus. You can find this answer in the last paragraph of the passage.

16. **(4)** The progress of Alzheimer's disease can be slowed by physical therapy and exercise. You can find this answer in the last paragraph of the passage.

17. **(2)** The BEST title for the passage is "Factors That Affect the Blood Alcohol Concentration." The passage describes the factors in paragraphs 2, 3, 4, and 5.

18. **(2)** The passage states that a 12-ounce beer contains the same amount of alcohol as $1\frac{1}{2}$ ounces of 86-proof whiskey. You can find this answer in the third paragraph of the passage.

19. **(3)** The person's age is NOT used to estimate BAC. You can find a list of the factors used to estimate BAC in the second and third paragraphs of the passage.

20. **(1)** The person that weighs less will have a higher BAC. You can find this answer in the fourth paragraph of the passage.

21. **(3)** The BEST title for this passage is "Repotting Houseplants." The passage tells you how to repot a houseplant that has outgrown its pot.

22. **(4)** A pot with a hole in it provides drainage. You can find this answer in the third paragraph of the passage.

23. **(2)** Clay is NOT an ingredient for potting soil. The ingredients for potting soil can be found in the fourth paragraph of the passage.

24. **(1)** After you remove a plant from its old pot, you should place the plant on a layer of fresh soil in the new pot. You can find this answer in the last paragraph of the passage.

Part B: Social Studies

1. **(4)** The main idea of the passage is that power under the federal system is divided between the states and the central government. You can find this answer in the first paragraph of the passage.

2. **(3)** The central government cannot become too powerful. The federal system restrains the power of the central government. You can find this answer in the third paragraph of the passage.

3. **(2)** The passage states that the central government CANNOT put a limit on the amount of money that a state taxes its people. You can find this answer in the second paragraph of the passage.

4. **(2)** The powers of the central government are assigned to it by the Constitution. You can find this answer in the first paragraph of the passage.

5. **(2)** The main purpose of this passage is to explain the practice of "quid pro quo." The deal between Morris and Blake is an example of "quid pro quo."

6. **(3)** There is unemployment in Morris's state because the coal business is suffering. You can find this answer in the second paragraph of the passage.

7. **(4)** Blake wanted the government to buy the farmers' extra crops. You can find this answer in the third paragraph of the passage.

8. **(1)** Blake agreed to vote for the jobs bill because Morris agreed to vote for the farm bill. This was practicing "quid pro quo." You can find this answer in the fifth paragraph of the passage.

9. **(3)** The main idea of the passage is that a political party is organized so that its goals and ideas can direct government's actions. A party raises funds and elects candidates with hopes of directing government's actions.

10. **(4)** A platform is a statement of goals. You can find this answer in the fourth paragraph of the passage.

11. **(1)** The major job of a party is to nominate candidates. You can find this answer in the fourth paragraph of the passage.

12. **(2)** A platform is a statement of goals. Different parties have different goals. Therefore, the two major parties do NOT often have the same platform. Paragraph 2 tells you that parties nominate candidates for office. Paragraph 5 states that parties use money from fund-raising to get their candidates elected. Paragraph 1 tells you that parties want their goals and ideas to direct government's actions.

13. **(1)** The central idea of the passage is that third parties are formed when a group is unhappy with the two major parties. The Populist Party is used as an example to support the main idea.

14. **(3)** The farmers were dissatisfied with the two major parties because the Democrats and Republicans did not agree with the farmers' goals. You can find this answer in the second paragraph of the passage.

15. **(2)** Reduced unemployment was NOT one of the farmers' goals mentioned in the passage. The farmers wanted an eight-hour work day, government control of the communication systems, and inflation of the currency. You can find this information in paragraph 3.

16. **(1)** Most people left the Populist Party to join the Democratic Party. You can find this answer in the fifth paragraph of the passage.

17. **(4)** The main idea of the passage is that a social institution is a set of beliefs, ideas, and rules. The passage explains the basics of social institutions.

18. **(2)** Social institutions do NOT separate people from their groups. Social institutions are ideas and rules that hold groups of people together (paragraph 1). The other statements about social institutions can be found in paragraphs 2 and 4.

19. **(3)** The point that divorce is more acceptable than it used to be is cited in the passage as an example of how the family has changed. You can find this answer in the fourth paragraph of the passage.

20. **(1)** The BEST title for the passage is "Social Institutions." The passage explains social institutions. The family is used as an example of a social institution.

21. **(1)** The main idea of the passage is that socialization is the way in which a person learns to live in a society. Minh's experiences in America are an example of resocialization.

22. **(2)** Minh did not understand why the elderly man and woman were not shopping with their children. In Vietnam, children help their parents. You can find this answer in the fourth paragraph of the passage.

23. **(4)** Everyone goes through the process of socialization. You can find this answer in the sixth paragraph of the passage.

24. **(2)** People stared at Minh and his friend because they were holding hands. People in America are not used to men holding hands. You can find this answer in the fifth paragraph of the passage.

Part C: Science

1. **(1)** The main idea of the passage is that photosynthesis is a process by which green plants produce glucose and release oxygen. This process is described in the passage.

2. **(3)** The three basic ingredients used in photosynthesis are water, sunlight, and carbon dioxide. You can find this answer in the fourth paragraph of the passage.

3. **(2)** When sunlight hits the leaves of a green plant, the chlorophyll in the plant absorbs the sunlight. You can find this answer in the fourth paragraph of the passage.

4. **(2)** Glucose is formed from hydrogen atoms and carbon dioxide. You can find this answer in the last paragraph of the passage.

5. **(2)** The main idea of the passage is that scientists in Florida are trying to create a hybrid tomato plant. The passage explains how the scientists are trying to create a plant that yields square tomatoes. They are trying to do it by creating a hybrid tomato plant.

6. **(3)** The passage states that genetics is the study of heredity. This information is stated in the second paragraph.

7. **(1)** Scientists can produce new strains of a tomato plant by cross-pollinating plants. This is stated at the beginning of the fourth paragraph in the passage.

8. **(4)** A hybrid is a new strain of a plant. You can find this definition in the fourth paragraph.

9. **(3)** The main idea of the passage is that testing using live animals is a widespread practice that is coming under attack. The first two paragraphs of the passage tell you that animal testing is widespread. The rest of the passage describes two tests that some people think are cruel to animals.

10. **(2)** In the Draize test, chemicals are put in rabbits' eyes. You can find this answer in the third paragraph of the passage.

11. **(1)** The purpose of the LD 50 test is to find out how poisonous a substance is. You can find this answer in the fourth paragraph of the passage.

12. **(2)** People who approve of the Draize and LD 50 tests feel that these tests are necessary to make sure that products are safe for humans. You can find this answer in the fifth paragraph of the passage.

13. **(1)** The main idea of the passage is that dioxin is a highly toxic substance. The toxic effects of dioxin are described throughout the passage.

14. **(3)** Most information about dioxin's effects on humans comes from research on industrial workers. You can find this answer in the third paragraph of the passage.

15. **(2)** According to the passage, dioxin first affects the skin. You can find this answer in the fourth paragraph of the passage.

16. **(2)** The passage states that scar tissue on the liver is dangerous because it prevents the blood from flowing freely through the liver. You can find this answer in the last paragraph.

17. **(2)** The main idea of the passage is that stress-related illnesses occur in the average worker more frequently than in the worker's boss. This idea is stated in the second paragraph of the passage. It is explained in paragraphs 3 and 4.

18. **(3)** Bad business decisions are NOT mentioned as a cause of stress. The fear of being fired and feelings that one's job is not important are given as causes in paragraph 3. Worries about the future is given as a cause of stress in the last paragraph of the passage.

19. **(1)** Some doctors say that short-term stress is good for the body. You can find this answer in the last paragraph of the passage.

20. **(1)** According to the passage, lack of self-confidence is related to a poor self-image. You can find this answer in the third paragraph.

21. **(1)** The main idea of the passage is that acid rain is a very serious pollution problem. This idea is stated in the first paragraph. The passage describes the harmful effects of acid rain.

22. **(3)** According to the passage, acid rain forms in the upper atmosphere. You can find this answer in the second paragraph of the passage.

23. **(4)** The passage states that industries reacted to air quality standards by building taller smokestacks. You can find this answer in the fourth paragraph of the passage.

24. **(1)** The passage does NOT say that acid rain poisons fish. Acid rain raises the level of acid in a lake. The fish die because the high levels of acid in the lake kills the plants, which supply the fish's oxygen, and the insects, which supply the fish's food. You can find this information in the second paragraph of the passage.

INTERPRETING WHAT YOU READ

PART A: GENERAL READING

Read each passage. Then chose the correct answer to each question that follows the passage.

New City police officer Ken Lindley has made eight drunk-driving arrests in the last month. No one was more intoxicated than the man he stopped near Echo Bridge.

"His name was Sal," Officer Lindley said. "When we pulled him over, he opened his door and fell flat on his face. He thought he was on the other side of town. When you see someone like Sal, you figure we must be saving some lives."

Police are pleased with the results of their crackdown. During the first month, they removed 210 drunk drivers from the road. Police plan to continue their efforts.

Last Saturday night, a roadblock was set up on Highway 9 near Exit 15. The location of the roadblock changes nightly. Officer Lindley and his partner James O'Brian stopped cars and handed out leaflets on the dangers of drunk-driving. As they walked through the lanes of cars, the officers looked for signs of intoxication.

"Bloodshot eyes are sometimes a giveaway," explained Officer O'Brian. "We also try to get them to talk. That way, we can listen for slurred speech or detect alcohol on their breath. If we suspect that they're drunk, we give them a breath test." Drivers who refuse to take a breath test are arrested immediately.

Though the delay slowed traffic, most drivers didn't mind the wait.

"I think this is a fine idea," said Carol Lentini, a lawyer. "If this gets some of the drunks off the road, I'm all for it."

1. Which of the following best expresses the main point of the passage?

    (1) The New City Police Department has begun a crackdown on drunk driving.
    (2) Bloodshot eyes and slurred speech show that a person is drunk.
    (3) Police in New City have arrested 210 drunk drivers.
    (4) Most drivers don't mind being stopped if it helps to make driving safer.

2. The passage implies that Carol Lentini was stopped on the road because

    (1) she was driving near Echo Bridge
    (2) she was helping drivers who had been arrested
    (3) she was intoxicated
    (4) she was part of a routine police check for drunk drivers

3. The passage implies that someone who refuses to take a breath test

    (1) proves to police that he is drunk
    (2) is breaking the law
    (3) is exercising one of his Constitutional rights
    (4) causes delays in traffic

24

"We're staying," says Sam Ferris. "This is home," adds his wife Ella Mae. Few people would like to call Vicksville home. Vicksville is covered with noxin.

Vicksville is the site of the Corbett Company's manufacturing plant. For 23 years, the Corbett Company had been making pesticides with noxin. Two years ago, the government called for a ban on noxin. It said that the chemical was dangerous to humans. Government officials tested the soil in Vicksville. There were high levels of noxin for one mile around the Corbett plant.

"Our grandchildren would get sick every time they visited," says Mrs. Ferris. "They would get rashes on their faces and hands. We thought it was maybe poison ivy. We even joked about it. We said they must be allergic to their grandma and grandpa."

Then one night, the Ferrises learned the truth about the rashes. They were watching TV. A news program reported the government ban on noxin. The program stated that noxin had been linked to skin irritations and other health problems.

The next day, the Corbett Company sent the Ferrises a letter. The letter said that the company would test for noxin in the soil around the plant and the Ferrises' home. The company claimed that it knew of no noxin outside the plant. But government tests were finished before the Corbett Company's tests. And the government found high levels of noxin in the soil.

Sam Ferris worked for the Corbett Company for 20 years. The company's pension plan let him buy a handsome home. Mr. Ferris and his wife use pension money for tours and cruises. They have their own boat and trailer. "I don't think the company knew noxin was dangerous," he says. "If the company knew it was dangerous, the company wouldn't have used it."

Meanwhile, the Ferrises will stay in Vicksville. "The grandchildren don't come see us any more. We go out and visit them."

4. From the information in the passage, you can conclude that the Ferrises' grandchildren got rashes because

    (1) there is noxin inside the Corbett Company plant
    (2) there is noxin in the soil outside the Ferrises' home
    (3) the children touched poison ivy
    (4) the children touched their grandfather

5. The passage implies that the Ferrises' grandchildren will no longer visit their grandparents because the Ferrises

    (1) live near soil poisoned with noxin
    (2) live too far away
    (3) like to be away on cruises
    (4) like to travel to their grandchildren's home

6. From the information in the passage, which of the following can you conclude about Vicksville?

    (1) It is a quiet town.
    (2) It may be an unsafe town to live in.
    (3) It will be closed by the federal government.
    (4) It may ask the federal government to close the Corbett Company.

A fire left three Elm City fire fighters in critical condition last night. Two other fire fighters suffered smoke inhalation in the blaze.

"With both trucks this never would have happened," said Fire Chief Ben Esposito. "But one of the trucks was off on a false alarm. Now maybe the city will change its mind about voice-alarm boxes."

At 8:00 PM last night, Engine Company #6 received a fire signal. The signal came from an alarm box at 83rd Street and Charles Avenue. The block of 83rd Street and Charles Avenue is filled with abandoned warehouses. The fire fighters had to check the floors of each building. No sign of fire was found.

Police are now checking the alarm box on 83rd and Charles for fingerprints. "Chances are they won't find the person who set off the alarm," Esposito said. "It's just too easy to pull the alarm and run. Voice-alarm boxes would cut down on this problem. If someone had to stop and call to the fire department, he'd think twice about making a false alarm."

Five minutes after Company #6 left for 83rd and Charles, the fire department received a call from Carson's Department Store. A blaze had started on the fourth floor of the store. Company #7 answered the call at once. Fire swept to the upper floors of the store. "Employees told us that plastics were kept there," said one fire fighter. "The smoke went from white to black. We had to wear gas masks then."

Company #7 radioed Company #6 for help. Twenty minutes later, Company #6 arrived as Tony Rinaci, fire fighter for Company #7, was being carried off on a stretcher.

"I knew his father," said Esposito. "And now Tony. It's terrible."

This morning, City Councilmember Gene Quist called a meeting. He demanded a review of the fire department's budget. "I do not care about the price of voice-alarm boxes. We cannot afford another fire like the one last night," he said.

7. From the information in the passage, you can conclude that Company #6 took 20 minutes to answer the call for help because it was

    (1)   making a false alarm
    (2)   answering a false alarm
    (3)   fighting a fire at 83rd and Charles
    (4)   not receiving the radio call

8. You can infer that the city council had not bought voice-alarm boxes because voice-alarm boxes are

    (1)   unsafe
    (2)   expensive
    (3)   used at 83rd Street and Charles Avenue
    (4)   used for false alarms

9. The passage implies that voice-alarm boxes would help to cut down the number of

    (1)   injuries to fire fighters in Elm City
    (2)   fires in Elm City
    (3)   false alarms in Elm City
    (4)   fire companies in Elm City

People in Thomasburg have known Roger and Mr. Otis for years. In the morning, Roger leads Mr. Otis to the post office. Then Roger guides him to the supermarket. On street corners Roger stops when traffic is moving. Mr. Otis likes to bend down and scratch Roger's ears.

Mr. Otis does not know it, but he and Roger resemble each other. Mr. Otis is slim with white hair. Roger is lean with a white coat.

"What's the matter, boy?" Mr. Otis asked Roger one morning. Roger had stopped at a street corner. He stood there a long time. Mr. Otis heard cars stop, then pass. He heard them stop and pass again. "Why can't we go, Roger?" Finally, Roger pulled Mr. Otis across the street.

Roger started doing other strange things. He would enter doors very slowly and carefully. He would growl at neighbors until they came very near. One day, Mr. Otis went to the park. He let Roger out of his harness. A boy asked to play with Roger. "Catch, boy!" The game of catch didn't last long. "He can't catch the ball," said the boy. "Maybe he doesn't feel well."

Mr. Otis took Roger to a veterinarian. "What's the matter with Roger?" asked Mr. Otis. The doctor smiled gently. "He has cataracts, Mr. Otis. It's common at his age. I can perform a cataract operation. His eyes will be like new. He'll look a little funny, though."

"Well, I don't care about that," said Mr. Otis.

Now, you can see Mr. Otis and Roger on the streets of Thomasburg. Mr. Otis is the one in dark glasses. Roger, trotting next to him, is the one in the specially-made goggles. "He's my best friend," says Mr. Otis. "And I hear he's my twin, too."

10. It can be inferred from the passage that Roger is a

(1) horse   (2) seeing-eye dog   (3) little boy   (4) blind man

11. The passage implies that Mr. Otis did not know that Roger was going blind because Mr. Otis

(1) does not care about Roger   (2) is too busy with his work
(3) wears dark glasses   (4) is blind himself

12. From the information in the passage, what can you conclude about the effects of Roger's cataract operation?

(1) Roger must now wear dark glasses.
(2) Roger must now walk more slowly.
(3) Roger can now see better.
(4) Roger cannot play catch.

13. Which of the following BEST expresses the main point of the passage?

(1) Roger is Mr. Otis's seeing-eye dog.
(2) People in Thomasburg have known Roger and Mr. Otis for years.
(3) Roger had a cataract operation.
(4) Mr. Otis and his dog Roger have a lot in common.

The latest trend in health care is happening *outside* hospitals. Many patients are no longer staying in the hospital after they have minor surgery. Instead, they are going either directly home or to a special "outpatient" facility.

One doctor feels that outpatient surgery may be healthier for the patient. Dr. Marjorie Evans is Director of Outpatient Care at North Town Medical Center. "Patients are relieved when they can leave the hospital right after surgery," Dr. Evans said. "They're more comfortable at home or at an outpatient facility. They may get better faster when they're relaxed." Dr. Evans added that outpatient surgery also takes the "ouch" out of hospital costs.

Dr. Evans doesn't think of outpatient surgery as a new wave in medicine. "The medical profession has been working for years to make outpatient care possible. Pain-killing drugs have been improved. They don't have the side-effects they once had. People don't need to stay in the hospital to take the drugs."

Dr. Stuart Howard, a surgeon at North Town Medical Center, likes the outpatient option. "I recommend it for some patients who have plastic or cosmetic surgery, or minor joint operations. My only suggestion is that outpatient facilities should be located near hospital emergency rooms. Outpatient care cannot be expected to replace emergency facilities."

"The hospital isn't the only place to get quality care," Dr. Evans says. "Outpatient facilities are run by experienced health-care workers. And for patients that return home after surgery, being with the family is often the best medicine."

14. From Dr. Evans's comments in the passage, you can infer that patients do not like to stay in hospitals because

   (1) patients must take more pain-killing drugs in hospitals than in outpatient facilities
   (2) meals are not as good in hospitals as in outpatient facilities
   (3) patients cannot relax easily in hospitals
   (4) hospitals do not provide quality care

15. From information in the passage, you can infer that people once needed to stay in hospitals when they took pain-killing drugs because the drugs

   (1) had to be given by doctors or nurses
   (2) had side effects that required hospital care
   (3) were not effective outside the hospital
   (4) could not kill pain

16. The passage implies that Dr. Howard thinks outpatient facilities should be near hospital emergency rooms because

   (1) minor joint operations always require emergency care
   (2) outpatient facilities cannot handle medical emergencies
   (3) outpatient facilities are run by inexperienced health-care workers
   (4) emergency rooms need assistance from health-care workers at outpatient facilities

17. The passage implies that, compared to care in hospitals, outpatient care is

   (1) cheaper   (2) safer
   (3) more professional (4) more exciting

The word is out. The Harmonic Clowns are back. And they're better than ever.

It's been 2½ years since the four harmonica-playing geniuses from Lima, Ohio, last performed in public. But fans of the group don't have much longer to wait. The Clowns are scheduled to give a nationally televised concert next month.

"We were getting kind of bored sitting around Lima," said Ellis Alexander, the leader of the group. "We decided that 2½ years was a long enough retirement."

Why did the Harmonic Clowns quit in the first place? Alexander explained that it was a combination of factors. "First of all, we were all getting tired of traveling from city to city. Three of us have families, and it's rough trying to be both a father and a traveling musician."

Alexander added that the group will perform fewer concerts than they had in the past. "This way," he said, "we can be home more often. But not too often."

Bobby Warner, at 58 the oldest member of the group, pointed out that the group improved since it last performed publicly. "We're not only 2½ years older, we're 2½ years better," he said. The group has added some new tunes to its list. "We want to go after the younger crowd," Warner explained.

At a recent rehearsal, the Harmonic Clowns proved that they hadn't lost anything. Their first hit, "Time for Love," sounded just as bubbly as it did 20 years ago. Alexander and Warner performed a duet of "The Beer Barrel Polka" that sounded incredible. As the rhythm section, "Hands" Martin and Dimmy Clark were as sharp as ever.

18. It can be inferred from the passage that the members of the Harmonic Clowns have been playing together for

(1) 58 years   (2) 20 years   (3) 2½ years   (4) 5 years

19. It can be inferred from the passage that before the Harmonic Clowns went into retirement, they

(1) traveled around the country often
(2) had their own TV show
(3) were losing popularity
(4) fought with one another often

20. You can infer from the passage that the author last heard the Harmonic Clowns play

(1) at Bobby Warner's home in Lima, Ohio   (2) on TV
(3) at a rehearsal   (4) at a concert

21. The BEST title for this passage is

(1) Harmonic Clowns' Concert Is a Big Hit
(2) "Time for Love" Puts Harmonic Clowns on Record Charts
(3) Harmonic Clowns Return to Lima
(4) Harmonic Clowns Come Out of Retirement

Check your answers on page 50.

PART B: PROSE LITERATURE

Read each passage. Then choose the correct answer to each question that follows the passage.

Jack used to curse the front yard as if it were a living thing. He was the man who lived with my grandmother for thirty years. He was not my grandfather, but an Italian who came down the road one day selling lots in Florida.

He was selling a vision of eternal oranges and sunshine door to door in a land where people ate apples and it rained a lot.

Jack stopped at my grandmother's house to sell her a lot just a stone's throw from downtown Miami, and he was delivering her whiskey a week later. He stayed for thirty years and Florida went on without him.

Jack hated the front yard because he thought it was against him. There had been a beautiful lawn there when Jack came along, but he let it wander off into nothing. He refused to water it or take care of it in any way.

Now the ground was so hard that it gave his car flat tires in the summer. The yard was always finding a nail to put in one of his tires or the car was always sinking out of sight in the winter when the rains came on.

The lawn had belonged to my grandfather who lived out the end of his life in an insane asylum. It had been his pride and joy and was said to be the place where his powers came from.

1. The narrator implies that the real reason Jack had problems with the lawn was that

    (1) the lawn was against him
    (2) the narrator's grandfather told the lawn what to do
    (3) the lawn was a living thing
    (4) Jack did not take care of the lawn

2. It can be inferred from the passage that when the narrator's grandfather owned the lawn, the lawn had been

    (1) muddy   (2) hard   (3) beautiful   (4) full of nails

3. Which of the following can be inferred from the passage about Jack and the narrator's grandmother?

    (1) They both hated the front lawn.
    (2) They lived in Florida.
    (3) They came from Italy.
    (4) They lived in the narrator's grandmother's house.

4. Which of the following would be the BEST title for the passage?

    (1) The Beautiful Lawn   (2) Jack and the Front Yard
    (3) Jack the Salesman   (4) My Grandmother and Grandfather

In Dexter there is a great whistle which is blown when a freeze threatens. It is known everywhere as Mr. Perkins' whistle. Now it sounded out in the clear night, blast after blast. Over the countryside lights appeared in the windows of the farms. Men and women ran out into the fields and covered up their plants with whatever they had, while Mr. Perkins' whistle blew and blew.

Jason Morton was not waked up by the great whistle. On he slept, his cavernous breathing like roars coming from a hollow tree. His right hand had been thrown out, from some deepness he must have dreamed, and lay stretched on the cold floor in the very center of a patch of moonlight which had moved across the room.

Sara felt herself waking. She knew that Mr. Perkins' whistle was blowing, what it meant — and that it now remained for her to get Jason and go out to the field. A soft laxity, an illusion of warmth, flowed stubbornly down her body, and for a few moments she continued to lie still.

Then she was sitting up and seizing her husband by the shoulders, without saying a word, rocking him back and forth. It took all her strength to wake him. He coughed, his roaring was over, and he sat up. He said nothing either, and they both sat with bent heads and listened for the whistle. After a silence it blew again, a long, rising blast.

Promptly Sara and Jason got out of bed. They were both fully dressed, because of the cold, and only needed to put on their shoes. Jason lighted the lantern, and Sara gathered the bedclothes over her arm and followed him out.

5. Which of the following BEST expresses the main point of the passage?

   (1) There is a great whistle in Dexter known as Mr. Perkins' whistle.
   (2) Men and women ran out into the fields.
   (3) Jason and Sara had to wake up to cover their plants.
   (4) Jason and Sara wanted to sleep all night.

6. You can infer that people cover up their plants to keep them from

   (1) getting too wet   (2) drying out
   (3) getting too little shade   (4) freezing

7. It can be inferred from the passage that Sara and Jason will use the bedclothes to cover

   (1) themselves   (2) their plants
   (3) their children   (4) Mr. Perkins' whistle

My mother sat down, crying. I had never seen her cry before. I looked at my father. He stood above my mother, holding her tightly by the shoulder.

I asked, "What's the matter, Mama?"

My father asked, "You know any of your brother's friends?"

I said, No, because I wanted to hear what he would say.

"They done robbed a store, whoever they is, and stabbed a man half to death. They say Caleb was with them."

"A boy named Arthur — Arthur something-or-other," said my mother, "he the one say Caleb was there."

"Do you know him?" my father asked.

I shook my head, No: for a different reason this time.

"They used to steal things — they used to steal things," said my mother, "look like they was a regular gang, and the cops say — the cops say — they used that store for a hiding place."

"The cops say!" said my father.

I had seen the cops in the store many times; they had always been perfectly friendly with the owner. "The store is closed," I said. I went over to my mother. "Mama — Mama — what they going to do if they find Caleb?" My mind had stopped, stuck, screaming, on the faces of white cops.

"They going to take him away," she said.

I looked at my father. "But Caleb don't steal! Caleb never stole nothing in his whole life!" My father said nothing. We heard footsteps on the stairs. Not one of us moved. But the steps stopped just below our landing. Then I realized that I would have to find Caleb and tell him not to come home.

8. From the information in the passage, you can infer that Caleb is the narrator's

   (1) father   (2) brother   (3) cousin   (4) friend

9. Which of the following statements about Caleb CANNOT be inferred from the passage?

   (1) Caleb was wanted by the police.
   (2) Caleb had a friend named Arthur.
   (3) Caleb stabbed a man.
   (4) Caleb's family didn't know where he was.

10. The passage implies that Caleb was in danger of being

   (1) stabbed   (2) robbed   (3) beaten   (4) arrested

It was on a bridge, one tremendous, April morning, that I knew I had fallen in love. Harriet and I were walking hand in hand. The bridge was the Pont Royal, just before us was the great *horloge,* high and lifted up, saying ten to ten; beyond this, the golden statue of Joan of Arc, with her sword uplifted. Harriet and I were silent, for we had been quarreling about something. Now, when I look back, I think we had reached that state when an affair must either end or become something more than an affair.

I looked sideways at Harriet's face, which was still. Her dark-blue eyes were narrowed against the sun, and her full, pink lips were still slightly sulky, like a child's. In those days, she hardly ever wore make-up. I was in my shirt sleeves. Her face made me want to laugh and run my hand over her short dark hair. I wanted to pull her to me and say, *Baby, don't be mad at me,* and at that moment something tugged at my heart and made me catch my breath. There were millions of people all around us, but I was alone with Harriet. She was alone with me. Never, in all my life, until that moment, had I been alone with anyone.

11. The author's main concern in the passage is to describe

(1) a quarrel
(2) a woman named Harriet
(3) the Pont Royal and the statue of Joan of Arc
(4) the feeling of falling in love

12. In the passage, the author implies that this is the first time that he had ever

(1) walked across the Pont Royal   (2) fallen in love
(3) held Harriet's hand   (4) fought with Harriet

13. Which of the following inferences about Harriet and the author can be made based on the passage?

(1) Harriet and the author liked to walk on bridges.
(2) Harriet and the author were having an affair.
(3) Harriet and the author quarreled often.
(4) Harriet and the author liked being with other people.

HELGA! DO NOT OPEN THIS DOOR! Since you were here last week, I bought a PUMA, for burglar protection. This is a huge cat, a cougar or a mountain lion, about four feet long, not including the tail. The man I bought it from told me it was fairly tame, but it is NOT! It has tried to attack both dogs, who are OK and are locked in the guest room. I myself have just gone down to my doctor's to have stitches taken in my face and neck and arms. This ferocious puma is wandering loose inside the house. The S.P.C.A. people are coming soon to capture it and take it away. I tried to call you and tell you not to come today, but you had already left. Whatever you do, if the S.P.C.A. has not come before you, DO NOT UNDER ANY CIRCUMSTANCES OPEN THIS DOOR!!

Well, naturally, this gave me considerable pause. Helga was obviously the blonde cleaning woman. But this was a Tuesday and she came on Wednesdays. Or she used to. But she could have changed her days.

I stroll around the outside of the house. But all of the curtains and drapes are drawn and I can't see in. As I pass the guest-room windows, the two dogs bark inside. So this much of the note on the door is true.

So I wander back to the front door and I think and I ponder. Is there really a puma in there or is this just another one of Hastings' big fat dirty lies?

14. From the passage, you can infer that the note was written by

    (1) the narrator of the passage   (2) a doctor
    (3) Hastings   (4) Helga

15. The note implies that Hastings had gone to the doctor because

    (1) he had an allergy to cats
    (2) he had been attacked by the puma
    (3) he had been attacked by burglars
    (4) he had fought with the S.P.C.A. people

16. Based on the passage, which of the following words most nearly describes the narrator's feelings about Hastings?

    (1) anger   (2) fear   (3) mistrust   (4) admiration

17. From the passage, you can infer that the narrator does not really believe that

    (1) Hastings has a cleaning woman
    (2) there is a puma in the house
    (3) the puma is dangerous
    (4) Hastings has locked the dogs in the guest room

Next day around lunchtime, Toni and Brenda picked Gary up at the shoe shop and took him out for a hamburger. Sitting on each side of him at the counter, talking into his left ear and his right ear, they got right to the topic. What it came down to was that he had been borrowing too much money.

Yes, said Toni gently, he'd been hitting Vern for a five-dollar bill here, ten there, once in a while twenty. He hadn't been going to work a full number of hours either. "Vern and Ida said this to you?" Gary asked.

"Gary," said Toni, "I don't think you realize Daddy's financial situation. He's got too much pride to tell you."

"He'd be furious if he knew we were talking to you about this," Brenda said, "but Dad isn't making a whole lot right now. He created a job so the parole board would help you get out."

"If you need ten dollars," said Toni, "Daddy will be there. But not just to buy a six-pack and then come home and sit around and drink beer."

18. Which of the following statements about Gary is supported by the passage?

    (1) Gary is Vern's son.   (2) Gary hates Vern.
    (3) Gary is irresponsible.   (4) Gary does not like Toni and Brenda.

19. Based on the information in the passage, you can infer that Vern has helped Gary to

    (1) get rich   (2) pay his bills
    (3) meet a girl   (4) get out of jail

20. From the information in the passage, you can infer that Toni and Brenda feel that Gary is

    (1) taking advantage of Vern   (2) working too hard
    (3) drinking too much   (4) stealing from Vern

21. Which of the following statements about Gary can be inferred from the passage?

    (1) Gary is working at the hamburger stand.
    (2) Gary is working for Vern.
    (3) Gary is working in a liquor store.
    (4) Gary is not working anywhere.

Check your answers on page 52.

PART C: SOCIAL STUDIES

Read each passage. Then choose the correct answer to each question that follows the passage.

Until 1800, the United States only stretched from the Atlantic Ocean to the Mississippi River. The Mississippi River was vital to the country. Americans sent furs, wheat, and tobacco down the river to the sea. From the sea, the goods were shipped to Europe.

Before the goods could reach the sea, they passed through the port of New Orleans. New Orleans was controlled by Spain. For a time, Spain had refused to let American goods pass through the city. Americans feared that Spain might close the port again.

In 1800, Spain secretly sold New Orleans to France. Spain also sold Louisiana to France. Louisiana was a huge amount of land, fully a third of the present-day United States. It reached from the Mississippi River to the Rocky Mountains. Napoleon, ruler of France, was glad to have Louisiana. He had fought wars in Europe to win land and power.

President Thomas Jefferson heard about Spain's secret sale. In 1803, he wrote a letter to the American ambassador to France. The letter described plans for war. It said America and England would fight France if France closed New Orleans. Jefferson wanted to frighten the French. He let the letter fall into the hands of a French official.

Napoleon read the letter. He thought about his wars in Europe. He was losing battles, and his soldiers needed weapons, food, and clothing. Napoleon offered to sell New Orleans and Louisiana to the United States.

Jefferson bought the land, but he hadn't consulted Congress. He didn't know if the sale was legal. The Constitution did not say whether or not a president could buy land. When Jefferson told Congress about the sale, he stressed the value of the land. He said he'd paid only $15 million, or three cents an acre. Jefferson reminded Congress that the United States housed a growing people. It would need more land. In December 1803, Congress ruled that the Louisiana Purchase was legal.

1. It can be inferred from the passage that Jefferson feared that Napoleon would

    (1) sell Louisiana to Spain
    (2) close New Orleans and make war on the United States
    (3) lose his wars in Europe
    (4) sell more furs, wheat, and tobacco than the United States

2. You can infer from the passage that Jefferson wrote the letter describing war plans to

    (1) get help from England
    (2) inform England of the United States' plans
    (3) make sure Napoleon did not close New Orleans
    (4) make Napoleon end his wars in Europe

3. The author implies that Congress ruled the Louisiana Purchase legal because

    (1) the Constitution said presidents could buy land
    (2) the Constitution said Congress could buy land
    (3) the sale was clearly legal
    (4) Congress wanted the valuable land

In 1854, Nebraska and Kansas were not yet states. They were territories. Congress had to make a decision. Congress had to decide if slavery could be allowed in these territories.

The country was split over this question. Most of the South said slavery should be allowed in the territories. Most of the North said that slavery shouldn't be allowed. It was a heated debate. Finally, Congress passed the Kansas-Nebraska Act. This act left the decision up to the territories themselves.

Before 1854, there were two major parties in America. The parties were the Whigs and the Democrats. Democrats supported states' rights. Whigs believed in a strong central government. Most Democrats supported the Kansas-Nebraska Act. And some Southern Whigs supported the act. But many Northern Whigs did not like it. These Whigs were small farmers who did not own slaves.

The people who opposed the new act called themselves Anti-Nebraska men. They decided to form their own party. A few Democrats joined them. Abolitionists joined the party, also. Abolitionists wanted to abolish, or end, slavery.

The Republican Party was born. The new party called for an end to slavery in Washington, D.C. The party also wanted slavery to be illegal in new territories. In 1856, the Republicans nominated their first presidential candidate. He lost the election to the Democrat James Buchanan. But in the next presidential election, the Republicans tried again and won. Abraham Lincoln was the first Republican president of the United States.

4. From the passage, you can infer that Congress left the slavery question up to the territories because

    (1) Congress thought that the territories would make a better decision
    (2) Congress did not know how to settle the slavery issue
    (3) the territories would then make slavery illegal
    (4) the territories would then make slavery legal

5. Which of the following inferences can be made about Northern Whigs from the passage?

    (1) Many Northern Whigs feared competition from large, slave-owning farms.
    (2) Most Northern Whigs joined the Democratic Party.
    (3) Many Northern Whigs supported the Kansas-Nebraska Act.
    (4) No Northern Whigs joined the Republican Party.

6. Which of the following would be the BEST title for the passage?

    (1) Democrats and Whigs
    (2) Slavery in the Territories
    (3) The Nebraska-Kansas Act
    (4) The Birth of the Republican Party

Before the 1930's, workers were only paid as long as they were "smart." If they were smart enough not to be ill, they were paid. If they were smart enough not to be injured, they were paid. And if they were very smart, they would find strength to work every day until they died. When people were not this "smart," they looked for help. Their families, private charities, and churches did what they could. All of these groups helped when the economy was healthy.

When the Depression hit, families, charities, and churches were weakened. And there was more need of them than ever before. Pat Cauley, a construction worker, kept a diary. Here is an entry from 1932: "Went to church. I said the family needed something to keep going. Got a nice sermon. Came home, pockets empty." Cauley's story was told by millions of others. Even when charities did help, people were not completely happy. People on soup lines did not starve. But their pride went hungry.

In 1933, Democrat Franklin Roosevelt became president. He said government should replace charities. Since people paid for government, government support was not charity. Government support was people's tax money at work. People could feel they deserved government support.

In 1935, Roosevelt signed the Social Security Act. The Social Security Act provided money for the elderly, the blind, and the handicapped. Workers benefitted, too. Workers who were ill or injured were to receive money. Families were to receive assistance when working fathers died. People laid off from work were to be helped until they found new jobs.

7. The passage implies that Pat Cauley wanted which of the following from his church?

   (1) a prayer   (2) a sermon
   (3) construction work (4) money

8. Which of the following statements about Social Security is supported by the passage?

   (1) Healthy, employed workers would receive Social Security.
   (2) When unemployed workers found jobs, they would pay taxes for Social Security.
   (3) People prefer charity to Social Security.
   (4) Social Security is paid for by private charities, families and churches.

9. Which of the following would be the BEST title for the passage?

   (1) Before Social Security
   (2) Families and Private Charities
   (3) People's Tax Money at Work
   (4) Pat Cauley, Construction Worker

10. From the information in the passage, you can conclude that workers before 1935 were

   (1) healthier than today's workers
   (2) worse off than today's workers
   (3) smarter than today's workers
   (4) more religious than today's workers

Economics is the study of trade and the distribution of goods. One of the most famous economists of the 1800's was Karl Marx. Marx studied capitalism, which is a system based on the principles of free trade and private ownership. Marx explored his ideas about capitalism in a book called *Das Kapital*.

Marx was born in 1818 in Europe. When he was a boy, most people worked on farms. People grew crops for themselves. They saw their work rewarded in food for their tables. Years after Marx finished school, people were working in factories. For 10 or 12 hours a day, workers put together pieces of machines. Sometimes the workers never saw the machine in one piece.

Marx called this problem "alienation." He believed that the workers felt alienated from their work. They did not feel a part of their work. They no longer knew what they were making, or why. Their jobs seemed meaningless.

Another problem Marx found with capitalism was "surplus value." Factory owners paid the workers wages and sold what the workers produced. The factory owner, or capitalist, as Marx called him, made a profit. Marx thought that capitalists would always give workers barely enough to live on. Capitalists would squeeze as much work out of the workers as possible and pocket the surplus value.

Marx wrote that the workers wouldn't be able to bear the effects of capitalism. He believed that the workers would seize power and share profits equally.

11. From the information in the passage, you can conclude that Marx thought that farm workers were better off than factory workers because farm workers

    (1) had food to eat
    (2) were not alienated from their work
    (3) could pocket the surplus value
    (4) never worked 10 or 12 hours a day

12. In the passage, the word "alienated" (line 11) most nearly means

    (1) "confused"   (2) "removed"
    (3) "frightened"   (4) "angered"

13. You can infer from the passage that Marx thought capitalists were mainly interested in

    (1) the quality of the products   (2) the quantity of the products
    (3) profits   (4) the workers' happiness

14. The passage implies that Marx thought that capitalists would

    (1) develop a system of free trade   (2) share profits with workers
    (3) lose their power to the workers   (4) always be rich and powerful

Most people agree that taxes must be paid. Government couldn't run without money. So people don't argue against taxes. They just argue about how taxes should be collected.

At present, the federal government works with a "progressive tax." The tax covers a percentage of people's wages. Not everyone pays the same percentage of his salary in taxes. Taxpayers fall into different "tax brackets" depending on their income. Poor people are in a low tax bracket. They pay the smallest percentage of income in taxes. Middle income workers pay a larger percentage than the poor. And the rich fall into the high tax brackets. Few rich people like the progressive tax.

The government took a poll. Among other people, the government talked to Ray Mathers and Eve Winick.

"Let's change to a flat rate tax," says Ray Mathers. "Everyone should be taxed the same percentage. It's fair. And it's easy to figure out." Mathers is president of Trig Computer Company. He makes over $80,000 a year.

"I don't want a flat rate income tax," says Eve Winick. Winick is a grammar school teacher. Her school is in a poor neighborhood. She makes $14,000 a year. "I don't care if it's easier to figure out. What I want to know is, would I pay less tax?" Winick worries about her students' parents. "Some of them can hardly support themselves. Why should they pay heavier taxes? They're the people who need government services."

Mathers thinks a flat rate would help in the long run. "The country could lower taxes after a while. See, if I paid fewer taxes, I'd save money. I'd put that money into my business and hire more people. Those people could pay taxes. Everybody would be better off."

15. Which of the following statements BEST expresses the main idea of the passage?

   (1) The progressive tax covers a percentage of people's wages.
   (2) The flat rate taxes everyone the same percentage.
   (3) There is a debate over two different types of taxation.
   (4) Ray Mathers and Eve Winick answered a government poll.

16. You can infer from the passage that the people who are presently supposed to pay the highest percentage of their income in taxes are the

   (1) rich   (2) middle class   (3) poor   (4) businessmen

17. You can infer that an *unstated* reason Mathers likes the flat rate tax is that

   (1) it is easy to figure out   (2) it is fair
   (3) he probably pays heavy taxes   (4) he is poor

18. You can infer that an *unstated* reason Winick does not want a flat rate tax is that

   (1) she might have to pay more taxes
   (2) she is rich
   (3) the flat rate tax is hard to figure out
   (4) the flat rate tax is unfair to the rich

In the 1890's, Pullman, Illinois, was a company town. It was built and owned by the Pullman Palace Car Company. The Pullman Palace Car Company was a leading maker of railroad cars. The company had built the town to house its factory workers.

The people who lived in Pullman depended on the Pullman company for everything. The Pullman company was the only employer in town. If you wanted to live in Pullman, you had to work for the Pullman company. Workers paid high rents for their housing in Pullman. They worked long hours in the factories.

In 1893, there was an economic panic in the United States. The Pullman Company sold fewer railroad cars. Business dropped off. The company decided to cut its costs. It did so by cutting the workers' wages. It cut the workers' wages by 25 to 40 percent.

The workers in Pullman fought the wage cut. They asked the president of the company, George Pullman, to rescind his decision to cut wages. When Pullman refused to change his mind, the workers went on strike.

The Pullman strike began on May 11, 1894. At first, the strike was not a major one. But then the Pullman strikers got some important support. On June 26, the American Railway Union called a boycott of all Pullman railway cars. Union members refused to work on trains that were made up of Pullman cars. The boycott halted railroad traffic out of Chicago.

On July 2, the federal government obtained a court order against the strike. But the strike continued. Two days later, federal troops were sent to Chicago. Soon after, the strike was broken, and the railway union leaders were jailed. The Pullman workers went back to work for lower wages.

19. Which of the following would be the BEST title for the passage?

(1) The Town of Pullman, Illinois
(2) The Pullman Strike of 1894
(3) Strikes of the American Railway Union
(4) The Pullman Palace Car Company

20. The word "rescind" (line 15) most nearly means to

(1) "take back"   (2) "increase"   (3) "regret"   (4) "resist"

21. The passage implies that railroad traffic out of Chicago was halted because

(1) federal troops searched each train
(2) strikers had built barricades against traffic
(3) union members refused to work on any trains
(4) trains out of Chicago included a lot of Pullman cars

22. The passage implies that union leaders were jailed because they

(1) damaged Pullman property
(2) damaged government property
(3) disobeyed the court's order to end the strike
(4) had refused to work on all trains

Watch out for Bob Green. You might see his face on a dollar bill some day.

Green is the son of an Air Force officer. His uncle was a state senator. "When Uncle Al came to dinner," says Bob, "there were great talks. I kept my ears open." When Bob was in high school, he campaigned for his uncle's re-election.

After high school and college, Bob got a law degree. He practiced law with a friend of his uncle's. One law case put Green in the local newspapers. He defended a woman who had owned a gun without a license. "Who can blame her?" said Green. "Our city is unsafe." After a few years, Green ran for city council. His uncle came out of retirement to endorse him. Green ran on a law-and-order platform. He said the other candidate was soft on crime. Green was elected.

Green served on the city council for four years. Then he wanted to run for Congress. His party would not support him, however. They said his visibility was too low. Not enough people knew who he was. Green returned to his law practice. He defended Ramco, a major steel corporation in his state. Ramco was accused of forcing out competition. The Ramco case made headlines, and it won Green a lot of important friends in the steel company. Soon afterwards, Bob announced his candidacy for Congress. He bought his own television and radio ads. Newspaper polls showed that he was popular. At the state convention, the party nominated Green. With party support, he won the election.

In the House, Green met Congressman Chet Ackley. Together they passed bills for their state. They called for public housing, roads, and bridges. Green ordered construction of a new steel suspension bridge that Ramco built.

Green is now a U.S. senator. He has been seen daily on televised law enforcement hearings. There are rumors Green will run for president in the not-too-distant future.

"Right now I'm committed to my job as a United States senator. But if the people of this country want me to serve them as president," Green says with a smile, "I won't refuse them."

23. It can be inferred from the passage that when Bob Green's Uncle Al came to dinner, the family talked about

   (1) local news   (2) Air Force tactics
   (3) politics   (4) business strategies

24. You can infer from the passage that all of the following were factors in Green's election to city council EXCEPT his

   (1) uncle's endorsement   (2) law degree
   (3) tough position on crime   (4) connection with the steel industry

25. The passage implies that an *unstated* source of aid to Green's election to Congress was

   (1) Chet Ackley   (2) Ramco
   (3) a TV and radio producer   (4) Green's father

Check your answers on page 54.

PART D: SCIENCE

Read each passage. Then choose the correct answer to each question that follows the passage.

The scientific theories of Isaac Newton (1642–1727) have shaped the course of modern science. Some of Newton's most important theories deal with force and motion. In science, the word "force" stands for the cause that makes objects move in a certain way. "Motion" stands for the movement of an object.

Suppose a ball is lying on the floor. As it lies on the floor, the ball isn't moving. It is "at rest." Will that ball suddenly begin to move? No, it won't. But suppose you were to push the ball across the floor. Then the ball would move. You would be supplying the force needed to put the ball into motion. This situation is an example of the first part of Newton's first law of motion. Newton proposed that every object tends to remain at rest unless it is acted upon by a force.

Now, picture the ball as it rolls across the floor. Newton proposed that an object will move at a constant speed unless it is acted upon by a force. This is the second part of Newton's first law of motion. If there were no force to act upon the ball, it would continue to roll along the floor. But there is a force that acts upon the ball. This force is friction. Friction is the force that resists an object when it moves over another object. The ball is rolling over the floor. The friction of the ball against the floor slows down the ball.

1. Which of the following is the BEST title for the passage?

   (1) Isaac Newton, the Father of Modern Science
   (2) Force
   (3) Movement in a Ball
   (4) Newton's First Law of Motion

2. Which of the following statements about friction is supported by the passage?

   (1) The speed at which an object moves can be affected by friction.
   (2) Objects tend to remain at rest because of friction.
   (3) Friction is the movement of an object over another object.
   (4) Friction makes electricity.

3. According to the passage, if force is applied to an object that is at rest, the object will

   (1) remain at rest   (2) move
   (3) stop moving at a constant speed (4) produce friction

4. According to the passage, if force is applied to an object that is moving at a constant speed, the object will

   (1) produce friction
   (2) continue to move at the same speed
   (3) stop moving at a constant speed
   (4) remain at rest

Powerful energy is contained in the nucleus, or center, of an atom. This kind of energy is called nuclear energy. For years, scientists have been studying how to release this energy. Nuclear energy can provide power for homes and factories.

Nuclear power plants produce energy through a process known as a "fission reaction." In a fission reaction, the nucleus of an atom is broken into two parts of nearly equal weight. Energy is released when the nucleus breaks up. Uranium atoms are used in nuclear power plants. The uranium atoms are exposed to neutrons. Neutrons are particles that are contained in the nucleus of an atom. When the neutrons hit the uranium atoms, they produce a fission reaction.

Nuclear energy can be released through another kind of reaction known as a "fusion reaction." In a fusion reaction, the nuclei of two or more atoms are fused, or joined, together. Energy is released when the nuclei are fused together. The energy from the earth's greatest power source, the sun, comes from fusion reactions.

Scientists are studying how to produce and control fusion reactions for use in power plants. They know that a fusion reactor could supply safer, more reliable nuclear energy. But there are many problems that must be solved before fusion reactions can be used successfully. One problem is that extremely high temperatures are needed to fuse nuclei. Another problem involves the amount of energy that is released in these reactions. Fusion reactions give off enough heat to melt the furnaces that contain them. Scientists must find an appropriate container for nuclear fusion reactions.

5. The passage implies that energy is released in fusion reactions in the form of

    (1) heat   (2) gas   (3) electricity   (4) uranium

6. Which of the following CANNOT be inferred about fusion reactions from the passage?

    (1) Uranium atoms are used in fusion reactions.
    (2) Fusion reactions are not used in nuclear power plants.
    (3) Fusion reactions take place on the sun.
    (4) In a fusion reaction, the centers of two or more atoms join together to form one atom.

7. It can be inferred from the passage that the appropriate container for a fusion reaction should be able to

    (1) withstand high temperatures   (2) ignite fusion reactions
    (3) split atoms into two parts   (4) collect heat from the sun

8. Which of the following conclusions about nuclear fusion energy can be drawn from the passage?

    (1) Power plants will begin to use fusion energy next year.
    (2) Energy from nuclear fusion is not as safe as energy from nuclear fission.
    (3) Scientists still don't know how to control energy from nuclear fusion.
    (4) All forms of nuclear energy are unsafe and should not be used.

Not all long-distance phone calls are made over phone wires. Today, phone wires are being replaced by fiber optics. Fiber optics make telephoning faster and easier than ever before.

In the past, telephone calls were made mostly over copper wires. Copper wires are heavy and bulky. Fiber optics are flexible, glass fibers. They are no thicker than a human hair. A wire cable is as thick as a man's arm. An optical fiber cable is as thick as a thumb.

Fiber optics transfer sound into light. First, a person speaks into a phone. The sound is changed into electrical impulses. A small laser changes the electrical impulses into coded bursts of light. The light is decoded back into electrical impulses at the telephone receiving station. Finally, the electrical impulses are changed into sounds again at the receiving telephone.

Optical fibers transmit calls much faster than copper wires can. The laser pulses with light as fast as 90 million times a second. At that speed, every word in a dictionary can be sent through a single fiber in a few seconds. Optical fibers also save space. A few fibers can carry more calls than thousands of strands of copper cable.

Optical fibers will be used for video as well as voice communications. And they will prove useful in computer-to-computer hookups. However, it will take years to replace existing wires.

9. Which of the following best expresses the main point of the passage?

    (1) Fiber optics are an improvement in communication systems.
    (2) Fiber optics are flexible, glass fibers.
    (3) Copper wires have been used in most phone systems.
    (4) A few optical fibers can carry thousands of phone calls.

10. Which of the following CANNOT be inferred about fiber cables from the passage?

    (1) They carry light waves.
    (2) They can be used in many forms of communication.
    (3) They are better than copper wires.
    (4) They are shorter than copper wires.

11. You can infer from the passage that a "cable" is

    (1) a copper wire that is used to carry phone calls
    (2) a group of wires or strands that are bundled together
    (3) a glass fiber that carries coded bursts of light
    (4) a laser that changes electrical impulses into light

12. You can infer from the passage that the word "transmit" (line 13) most nearly means

    (1) "carry from one place to another"   (2) "pulse with light"
    (3) "operate quickly"   (4) "speak"

Suppose that you are watching a pot of water on a stove. There is a glass cover on the pot. A low flame is heating the water. What happens as the water heats up? Steam forms in the pot. And when the steam hits the cooler lid of the pot, the steam condenses. It forms drops of water. It may seem as though there is less water. But there isn't. The water simply changes form from liquid to vapor and back to liquid again.

The water cycle of the earth works on the same principle. When the sun warms the oceans, some of the ocean water becomes water vapor. The air holds the water vapor. As water vapor is carried up into the atmosphere, it hits cooler air. Cool air can't hold as much vapor. The vapor condenses into water droplets. The droplets form clouds. When conditions are right, the water from the clouds falls back to the earth as rain.

The oceans hold most of the earth's water. But water is held in rivers and lakes as well. Pockets of water are also contained in the ground. Winds carry moist, heavy air from the oceans over land. When it rains, much of the water is absorbed by the ground. Any excess water is carried through underground streams to lakes, rivers, and oceans. Some of the rainwater falls directly into lakes and rivers. Water from these sources may flow back into the ocean. Some of it is warmed and turns into vapor before it reaches the ocean. All of the earth's water takes part in the water cycle.

13. Which of the following is the BEST title for the passage?

   (1) Water Vapor   (2) Ocean Water
   (3) Water and Heat   (4) The Water Cycle

14. Which of the following statements about the water cycle CANNOT be inferred from the passage?

   (1) Lakes and rivers don't hold as much water as oceans do.
   (2) Water vapor condenses when it hits cooler air.
   (3) All rainwater comes from the oceans.
   (4) Clouds are made up of droplets of water.

15. From the information in the passage, you can infer that the flame under a pot is like the sun on the ocean because both

   (1) hold water vapor
   (2) condense vapor into water droplets
   (3) change water to water vapor
   (4) cause clouds to form

16. By comparing the earth's water cycle to the pot on the stove, the author is showing that the amount of water in the water cycle

   (1) does not change a lot
   (2) decreases a lot every time it goes through the water cycle
   (3) decreases a little every time it goes through the water cycle
   (4) increases a little every time it goes through the water cycle

There's no way for oil explorers to be sure that they're going to strike oil when they drill for it. But the science of geology has helped to increase the chances of striking oil.

Geology is the science that deals with the earth and rock formation. There are several types of rock formations that hold oil. But these formations are only present deep below the earth's surface. Geologists have had to find ways of "seeing" thousands of feet down into the earth.

The geologist's most useful tool is the seismograph. The seismograph was invented to detect and measure earthquakes. To use the seismograph to find oil, the geologist creates his own miniature earthquakes. These artificial earthquakes are caused by setting off charges of dynamite. The dynamite is buried deep in the ground. When the dynamite is set off, the explosion sends shock waves through the layers of rock and earth below.

When the shock waves strike layers of rock, they bounce back to the surface. The strength of the returning shock is measured on the seismograph. These measurements tell the geologist whether the rock is hard or soft. If the rock is soft, the returning vibrations will be weak. Weak vibrations tell the geologist that the rock may hold oil.

The time it takes for the vibrations to return to the surface is also important. The longer it takes for the shock to return, the deeper the rock formation is. By taking many seismograph soundings over a wide area, the geologist can make a map of underground rock formations.

17. According to information in the passage, you can infer that chances of striking oil have increased because geologists

    (1) have learned to use earthquakes to find oil
    (2) have invented better oil drills
    (3) now use seismographs to predict where oil is
    (4) now know where all the earth's oil is

18. Which of the following can be inferred about rock, vibrations, and oil based on information in the passage?

    (1) Soft rock returns weak vibrations and may hold oil.
    (2) Soft rock returns strong vibrations and may hold oil.
    (3) Hard rock returns weak vibrations and may hold oil.
    (4) Hard rock returns strong vibrations and may hold oil.

19. Which of the following would be the BEST title for the passage?

    (1) Better Odds for Striking Oil
    (2) How Seismographs Strike Oil
    (3) How Seismographs Help Search for Oil
    (4) How Geologists Dig for Oil

20. Which of the following kinds of vibrations would tell a geologist that no oil is present underground?

    (1) a strong vibration
    (2) a weak vibration
    (3) a vibration that takes a long time to return
    (4) a vibration that takes a short time to return

Animals that don't have backbones are known as invertebrates. Invertebrates make up 95 percent of all animal life on earth. They range in size from tiny one-celled amoebas to larger animals, such as lobsters and crabs.

Invertebrates fall into two categories: protozoa and metazoa. Protozoa are one-celled animals. Their bodies have no fixed form. They have no skeleton at all. Metazoa are multi-celled animals. All metazoa have fixed forms. Some invertebrate metazoa, such as snails, have a hard shell. This shell acts as an external skeleton. It is called an exoskeleton.

Vertebrates are multi-celled animals that have backbones. Their backbone is part of their internal skeleton. The backbone, or spine, helps protect the vertebrate's nervous system. The spine runs down the center of the animal's body. The left side of the vertebrate's body is the same as the right side. This means that all vertebrates are bilaterally symmetrical. In addition, all vertebrates have a brain that is enclosed in a bony skull. They all have complex internal systems, and the parts of the system are developed to do specific jobs.

21. According to information in the passage, all of the following describe invertebrates EXCEPT:

   (1) They are the largest group of animal life on earth.
   (2) They are one-celled animals.
   (3) They do not all look alike.
   (4) They don't all have skeletons.

22. The word "bilaterally" (line 13) most nearly means

   (1) "complex"   (2) "one-sided"
   (3) "divided into two sides"   (4) enclosed in a bony skull"

23. The passage implies that the main difference between vertebrates and invertebrates is that invertebrates do NOT have

   (1) a backbone   (2) a skeleton
   (3) a brain   (4) a nervous system

24. The passage implies that one main difference between protozoa and metazoa is that protozoa do NOT have

   (1) any cells   (2) a fixed form
   (3) an internal skeleton (4) a nervous system

Medicine comes in many forms. In its liquid form, medicine affects the body very quickly. But the effects of liquid medicine aren't usually long-lasting. That is why pills and capsules are also used.

The pills and capsules being sold today aren't perfect, either. Pills dissolve in the stomach. The medicine in the pills is released when the pills dissolve. But often, the pills dissolve too quickly.

Scientists have been trying to develop a pill that can release medicine slowly over a long period of time. They have applied their knowledge of plants to produce the "osmotic pump pill."

The cell walls of plants are made of cellulose. Cellulose is a very porous substance. There are millions of tiny holes, or pores, in the cellulose walls of plants. These holes are big enough to allow water through the cell walls. As water enters a cell, pressure builds up in the cell. The pressure pumps other substances out of the cell. These substances leave the cell through the cellulose wall. This slow, steady process is called osmosis.

The osmotic pump pill is coated with synthetic cellulose. Liquid medicine is contained in the pill. The holes in the cellulose coating of the pill are big enough to allow water in the pill. As water from the body enters the pill, pressure builds up in the pill. The medicine is then slowly pumped out of the pill.

25. The passage implies that the osmotic pump pill is better than other pills and capsules because

    (1) it releases medicine slowly over a long period of time
    (2) the coating doesn't dissolve in the stomach
    (3) the medicine in the pill can affect the body quickly
    (4) it helps to build pressure in the body

26. The way that the osmotic pump pill works is based on a process called

    (1) cellulose   (2) osmosis   (3) pressure   (4) synthesis

27. The passage implies that medicine in an osmotic pump pill will leave the pill when

    (1) the pill is swallowed
    (2) the cellulose coating is dissolved
    (3) enough pressure builds up in the pill
    (4) the medicine is dissolved with water from the body

28. The passage implies that cellulose is a very porous substance because it contains

    (1) millions of tiny holes
    (2) a substance that dissolves it
    (3) a substance that creates pressure
    (4) liquid medicine

Check your answers on page 56.

ANSWERS AND EXPLANATIONS

Part A: General Reading

1. **(1)** The main point of the passage is that the New City Police Department has begun a crackdown on drunk driving. The passage describes the crackdown and gives you several people's opinion of it.

2. **(4)** The passage implies that Carol Lentini was stopped on the road because she was part of a routine police check for drunk drivers. Paragraph 4 tells you that police set up a roadblock to check for drunk drivers. Paragraph 6 says that most drivers didn't mind waiting in the roadblock. Carol Lentini is quoted as one of those drivers.

3. **(2)** The passage implies that someone who refuses to take a breath test is breaking the law. Paragraph 5 tells you that someone who refuses to take a breath test is arrested immediately.

4. **(2)** You can conclude that the Ferrises' grandchildren got rashes because there is noxin in the soil outside the Ferrises' home. The fifth paragraph tells you that there is noxin in the soil outside the Ferrises' home. The fourth paragraph tells you that noxin causes skin irritations, or rashes.

5. **(1)** The passage implies that the Ferrises' grandchildren will no longer visit their grandparents because the Ferrises live near soil poisoned with noxin. Paragraph 5 tells you that the Ferrises' live near soil poisoned with noxin. Paragraph 3 tells you that the Ferrises' grandchildren got sick when they visited the Ferrises. Paragraph 4 tells you that noxin can make you sick.

6. **(2)** You can conclude that Vicksville may be an unsafe town to live in. The first paragraph tells you that Vicksville is covered with noxin. The second paragraph tells you that noxin is dangerous to humans.

7. **(2)** You can conclude that Company #6 took 20 minutes to answer the call for help because it was answering a false alarm. The second paragraph tells you that at the time of the fire, one of the trucks was off on a false alarm. The third paragraph tells you that Company #6 was off on a false alarm.

8. **(2)** You can infer that the city council had not bought voice-alarm boxes because voice-alarm boxes are expensive. In the last paragraph, a city councilmember says that the price of voice-alarm boxes should not stop the city from buying them.

9. **(3)** The passage implies that voice-alarm boxes would help to cut down the number of false alarms in Elm City. In paragraph 4, Chief Esposito says that if a person had to stop and call the fire department, he'd think twice about making a false alarm.

10. **(2)** You can infer that Roger is a seeing-eye dog. The fifth paragraph tells you that Roger was taken to a veterinarian. This shows that he is an animal. The first and third paragraphs tell you that Roger guided Mr. Otis in the way that seeing-eye dogs guide the blind.

11. **(4)** The passage implies that Mr. Otis did not know Roger was going blind because Mr. Otis was blind himself. The first paragraph tells you that Mr. Otis had to be guided on his walks. The second paragraph tells you that he didn't know what Roger looked like. These clues tell you that Mr. Otis was blind.

12. **(3)** You can conclude that one effect of Roger's cataract operation was that he can now see better. In the fifth paragraph, the veterinarian says that Roger's eyes will be like new. In the last paragraph, the author shows you that Roger is still guiding Mr. Otis.

13. **(4)** The main point of the passage is that Mr. Otis and his dog Roger have a lot in common. The first and second paragraphs give clues that Mr. Otis was blind. The third and fourth paragraphs gives clues that Roger is no longer seeing well. The second paragraph tells that Roger looks a little like Mr. Otis.

14. **(3)** You can infer that patients do not like to stay in hospitals because they cannot relax easily in hospitals. In the second paragraph, Dr. Evans tells you that patients may get better faster outside the hospital because they're more relaxed.

15. **(2)** You can conclude that people once needed to stay in hospitals when they took pain-killing drugs because the drugs had side effects that required hospital care. In the third paragraph, Dr. Evans tells you that the new drugs don't have the side effects they once had.

16. **(2)** The passage implies that Dr. Howard thinks that outpatient facilities should be near hospital emergency rooms because outpatient facilities cannot handle medical emergencies. In the fourth paragraph, Dr. Howard tells you that outpatient care cannot replace emergency facilities.

17. **(1)** The passage implies that, compared to care in hospitals, outpatient care is cheaper. In the second paragraph, Dr. Evans tells you that outpatient surgery takes the "ouch" out of hospital costs. This tells you that hospital care costs more than outpatient care.

18. **(2)** You can infer that the members of the Harmonic Clowns have been playing together for 20 years. The last paragraph tells you that they had their first hit twenty years ago.

19. **(1)** You can conclude that before the Harmonic Clowns went into retirement, they traveled around the country often. In the fourth paragraph, Ellis Alexander tells you that they were tired of traveling from city to city.

20. **(3)** You can infer that the author last heard the Harmonic Clowns play at a rehearsal. The last paragraph tells you that the author heard the Clowns play at a recent rehearsal.

21. **(4)** The BEST title for the passage is "Harmonic Clowns Come Out of Retirement." The first paragraph tells you that the Harmonic Clowns are back. The third paragraph tells you that their retirement had been long enough.

Part B: Prose Literature

1. **(4)** The narrator implies that the real reason Jack had trouble with the lawn was that he didn't take care of it. Paragraph 4 tells you that the lawn had been beautiful when Jack arrived, but he refused to take care of it.

2. **(3)** It can be inferred that when the narrator's grandfather owned the lawn, the lawn had been beautiful. The last paragraph tells you that the lawn was the narrator's grandfather's pride and joy. The fourth paragraph tells you that the lawn was still beautiful when Jack arrived.

3. **(4)** It can be inferred that Jack and the narrator's grandmother lived in the grandmother's house. Paragraph 3 tells you that Jack had stopped at her house and had stayed for thirty years.

4. **(2)** The BEST title for the passage would be "Jack and the Front Yard." The passage describes Jack and his feelings about the yard.

5. **(3)** The main point of the passage is that Jason and Sara had to wake up and cover their plants. The first paragraph describes how the people of Dexter have to cover their plants when there is frost. A whistle signals that frost is coming. The rest of the passage is about how Sara and Jason woke up to the whistle.

6. **(4)** You can infer that people cover up their plants to keep them from freezing. The first paragraph tells you that when a freeze threatens, men and women run out into the fields and cover up their plants.

7. **(2)** It can be inferred that Jason and Sara will use the bedclothes to cover their plants. The whistle told Sara that there was a freeze coming (paragraph 3). The first paragraph says that people cover their plants with whatever they have when a freeze is coming.

8. **(2)** You can infer that Caleb is the narrator's brother. The entire conversation is about Caleb and his friends. In paragraph 3, the narrator's father asks the narrator if he knows any of his brother's friends.

9. **(3)** You CANNOT infer from the passage that Caleb stabbed a man. Paragraph 5 says that a man was stabbed and that the police say that Caleb was there. It does not say that Caleb was the one who stabbed the man.

10. **(4)** The passage implies that Caleb was in danger of being arrested. The passage tells you that the police are looking for Caleb. The narrator's mother says the police will take him away. From this, you can infer that Caleb is in danger of being arrested.

11. **(4)** The author's main concern is to describe the feeling of falling in love. In the first sentence, the author tells you that he had fallen in love. In the rest of the passage the author describes his feelings.

12. **(2)** The author implies that this is the first time he had ever fallen in love. In the last sentence, the author says that he had never felt alone with anyone before. The author implies that this feeling is love.

13. **(2)** You can infer that Harriet and the author were having an affair. In the first paragraph, the author says that they had reached an important point in their affair.

14. **(3)** You can infer that the note was written by Hastings. In the last paragraph, the author wonders if the note is another one of Hastings' lies. This links the note to Hastings.

15. **(2)** The note implies that Hastings had gone to the doctor because he had been attacked by the puma. The note says that the puma tried to attack Hastings' dogs. The note also describes how dangerous the puma is. It says that Hastings is going to the doctor to get stitches.

16. **(3)** "Mistrust" most nearly describes the narrator's feelings about Hastings. In the last paragraph, the narrator implies that Hastings is a liar.

17. **(2)** You can infer that the narrator does not really believe that there is a puma in the house. In the third paragraph, the narrator tries to look for the puma in the house. In the last paragraph, the narrator expresses doubt that the note is true.

18. **(3)** The passage supports the statement that Gary is irresponsible. In the first paragraph, Toni and Brenda have to tell Gary that he had been borrowing too much money. The last paragraph tells you that Gary was only using the money to buy beer.

19. **(4)** You can infer that Vern has helped Gary to get out of jail. Paragraph 4 tells you that Vern created a job for Gary so the parole board would help Gary get out.

20. **(1)** You can infer that Toni and Brenda feel that Gary is taking advantage of Vern. The second paragraph tells you Gary has been borrowing money from Vern. It also tells you that Gary hadn't been working hard at the job Vern gave him.

21. **(2)** You can infer that Gary is working for Vern. In the fourth paragraph, Brenda says that Vern created a job for Gary.

Part C: Social Studies

1. **(2)** It can be inferred from the passage that Jefferson feared that Napoleon would close New Orleans and make war on the United States. The fourth paragraph tells you that Jefferson wrote a letter stating that the U.S. would fight France if Napoleon closed New Orleans. The third paragraph states that Napoleon fought wars to win land and power.

2. **(3)** You can infer from the passage that Jefferson wrote the letter describing war plans to make sure that Napoleon did not close New Orleans. Paragraph 4 tells you that the letter said that America would fight France if the port was closed. The paragraph tells you that Jefferson wanted to frighten the French with the letter.

3. **(4)** The author implies that Congress ruled the Louisiana Purchase legal because Congress wanted the valuable land. In the last paragraph, the author says that Jefferson stressed the value of the land to Congress.

4. **(2)** You can infer that Congress left the slavery question up to the territories because Congress did not know how to settle the slavery issue. Paragraph 2 tells you that the country was split over the slavery issue. Congress couldn't agree about slavery, so they left the decision to the territories.

5. **(1)** You can infer from the passage that most Northern Whigs feared competition from large, slave-owning farms. Paragraph 3 tells you that these Whigs had small farms. They did not own slaves. They were against the Kansas-Nebraska Act. You can infer from this information that Northern Whigs feared competition from slave-owners in the territories.

6. **(4)** The BEST title for the passage is "The Birth of the Republican Party." The first three paragraphs tell you the issues that lead to the formation of the Republican Party. The fourth paragraph tells you who joined the party. The fifth paragraph tells you about the party's first candidates.

7. **(4)** The passage implies that Pat Cauley wanted money from his church. In Cauley's diary entry (paragraph 3), Cauley says that he went to church and asked for something to "keep going." It is implied that Cauley wanted money because he complains that he returned from church with "empty pockets."

8. **(2)** The passage supports the statement that when unemployed workers found jobs, they would pay taxes for Social Security. Paragraph 4 tells you that government support is people's tax money at work. Taxes on workers' income go to government programs like Social Security.

9. **(1)** The BEST title for the passage is "Before Social Security." The passage tells you about the conditions that lead up to the Social Security Act.

10. **(2)** From the information in the passage, you can conclude that workers before 1935 were worse off than today's workers. The passage tells you that workers before 1935 could not count on any government help if they were injured on the job or laid off.

11. **(2)** From the information in the passage, you can conclude that Marx thought that farm workers were better off than factory workers because farm workers were not alienated from their work. Paragraph 2 states that farm workers saw their work rewarded in food for their tables. Factory workers, however, often didn't see the end product of their work. Marx said that this made the factory workers feel alienated (paragraph 3).

12. **(2)** The word "alienated" (line 11) most nearly means "removed." The second sentence in paragraph 3 tells you that workers felt alienated from their work. The next sentence explains how the workers felt. It says that they didn't feel a part of their work. From this you can figure out that "alienated" means "removed."

13. **(3)** You can infer from the passage that Marx thought capitalists were mainly interested in profits. Paragraph 4 tells you that Marx thought capitalists would squeeze as much work out of the workers as possible and pocket the profits.

14. **(3)** The passage implies that Marx thought capitalists would lose their power to the workers. The last paragraph tells you that Marx thought that workers would seize power. The capitalists would lose their power if this happened.

15. **(3)** The main idea of the passage is that there is a debate over two different types of taxation. The passage describes the two different types of taxation, and it gives two people's differing opinions on these methods of taxing.

16. **(1)** You can infer that the people who are supposed to pay the highest percentage of their income in taxes are the rich. The second paragraph tells you that people pay different percentages of their salary in taxes depending on their income bracket. The poor pay a low percentage and are in a low income bracket. Therefore, the rich, who are in a high income bracket, pay a high percentage.

17. **(3)** An unstated reason Mathers likes the flat rate tax is that he probably pays heavy taxes. The fourth paragraph tells you that he makes over $80,000 a year. That income puts Mathers in a high tax bracket. You can also infer from paragraph 6 that Mathers thinks he would pay fewer taxes with a flat rate tax.

18. **(1)** An unstated reason why Winick doesn't want a flat rate tax is that she might have to pay more taxes. Paragraph 5 tells you that Winick thinks that people who aren't rich would have to pay more taxes with a flat rate tax. Since Winick makes $14,000 a year, she too would have to pay more taxes.

19. **(2)** The best title for the passage would be "The Pullman Strike of 1894." The passage describes the history of the strike.

20. **(1)** The word "rescind" (line 15) most nearly means to "take back." The second sentence in paragraph 4 tells you that the workers asked Pullman to rescind his decision. The next sentence tells you that Pullman wouldn't "change his mind." He wouldn't "take back" his decision.

21. **(4)** The passage implies that railroad traffic out of Chicago was halted because trains out of Chicago included a lot of Pullman cars. Paragraph 5 tells you that railway workers halted work on trains with Pullman cars. You can infer that trains out of Chicago must have carried a lot of Pullman cars.

22. **(3)** The passage implies that union leaders were jailed because they disobeyed the court's order to end the strike. The last paragraph tells you that there was a court order to end the strike. The union, however, disobeyed the order and continued the strike.

23. **(3)** It can be inferred that when Bob Green's Uncle Al came to dinner, the family talked about politics. The second paragraph is about how Green became interested in politics. It tells you that Uncle Al was a state senator. You can infer that Uncle Al talked about politics at family dinners.

24. **(4)** You can infer that Green's connection with the steel industry was not a factor in his election to city council. Paragraph 4 tells you that Green didn't get involved with the steel industry until after he left the city council.

25. **(2)** The passage implies that an unstated source of aid to Green's election to Congress was Ramco. Paragraph 4 tells you that Green made a lot of important friends at Ramco. Paragraph 5 tells you that after Green was elected, Ramco got a contract for a big suspension bridge. You can infer from this information that Green and Ramco were helping each other.

Part D: Science

1. **(4)** The BEST title for the passage is "Newton's First Law of Motion." The passage describes Newton's first law of motion. The movement of a ball is used to illustrate the law.

2. **(1)** The passage supports the statement that the speed at which an object moves can be affected by friction. Paragraph 3 tells you that an object will move at a constant speed unless it's acted upon by a force. The paragraph also tells you that friction is a force that can act upon a moving object.

3. **(2)** You can conclude that when force is applied to an object that is at rest, the object will move. The second paragraph describes a ball at rest. It tells you that if you pushed the ball, the ball would move. The paragraph tells you that force would make the ball move.

4. **(3)** You can infer that if force is applied to an object that is moving at a constant speed, the object will stop moving at a constant speed. The third paragraph tells you that an object will move at a constant speed unless it is acted upon by a force. You can infer that the object will no longer move at the constant speed when force is applied.

5. **(1)** The passage implies that energy is released in fusion reactions in the form of heat. The last paragraph tells you that fusion reactions give off enough heat to melt the furnaces that contain them.

6. **(1)** From the passage, you CANNOT infer that uranium atoms are used in fusion reactions. The third paragraph tells you that the nuclei of two or more atoms are fused together. It doesn't tell you what kind of atoms are fused.

7. **(1)** You can infer from the passage that the appropriate container for a fusion reaction should be able to withstand high temperatures. The last paragraph tells you that fusion reactions give off enough heat to melt the furnaces that contain them. You can infer that the appropriate container must be able to withstand a high degree of heat.

8. **(3)** You can conclude that scientists still don't know how to control energy from nuclear fusion. The last paragraph tells you that scientists have not yet found an appropriate container for fusion reactions. This tells you that scientists cannot yet successfully control nuclear fusion reactions.

9. **(1)** The main point of the passage is that fiber optics are an improvement in communication systems. The first paragraph tells you that fiber optics make telephoning faster and easier than before. The rest of the passage describes the way fiber optics work.

10. **(4)** From the passage, you CANNOT infer that fiber cables are shorter than copper wires. There is nothing in the passage about the length of fiber cables.

11. **(2)** You can infer that a "cable" is a group of wires or strands that are bundled together. Paragraph 2 tells you that a fiber strand is no thicker than a human hair. It tells you that a fiber cable is as thick as a thumb. From this you can infer that a cable is made up of many wires or strands.

12. **(1)** You can infer that the word "transmit" (line 13) most nearly means to "carry from one place to another." The first sentence in paragraph 4 tells you that both optical fibers and copper wires "transmit" calls. The last sentence in the paragraph tells you that fibers and wires "carry" calls. Since you know that phone cables carry calls "from one place to another," you can figure out what "transmit" means.

13. **(4)** The BEST title for the passage is "The Water Cycle." The passage describes the water cycle.

14. **(3)** The statement that all rainwater comes from the oceans CANNOT be inferred from the passage. The third paragraph tells you that some water from lakes and rivers turns into vapor before it reaches the ocean. You can infer that some of this vapor may turn into rainwater.

15. **(3)** You can infer that the flame under a pot is like the sun on the ocean because both change water to water vapor. The first paragraph tells you that a flame under a pot changes water into steam. Steam is water vapor. The second paragraph tells you that when the sun warms the ocean, some of the ocean water becomes water vapor.

16. **(1)** By comparing the earth's water cycle to the pot on the stove, the author is showing that the amount of water in the water cycle does not change a lot. In the first paragraph, the author says that there may seem to be less water in the pot, but there isn't. The water in the pot just changes form.

17. **(3)** You can infer that there are better chances of striking oil because geologists now use seismographs to predict where oil is. The third paragraph tells you that geologists use seismographs to find oil.

18. **(1)** You can infer that soft rock returns weak vibrations and may hold oil. The fifth paragraph tells you that if rock is soft, the returning vibrations will be weak. Weak vibrations tell the geologist that the rock may hold oil.

19. **(3)** The BEST title for the passage is "How Seismographs Help Search for Oil." The passage describes how the seismograph helps geologists predict where oil might be.

20. **(1)** The passage implies that a strong vibration would tell a geologist that there is no oil underground. The fifth paragraph tells you that weak vibrations tell geologists that the rock may hold oil. You can infer that strong vibrations tell geologists that there is no oil underground.

21. **(2)** The passage implies that invertebrates are NOT all one-celled. The second paragraph tells you that invertebrates are divided into protozoa and metazoa. Metazoa are described as multi-celled animals.

22. **(3)** The word "bilaterally" most nearly means "divided into two sides." The third paragraph tells you that the spine runs down the center of a vertebrate's body. The spine divides the body into a left side and a right side. From these clues, you can figure out that "bilateral" means "divided into two sides."

23. **(1)** The passage implies that the main difference between vertebrates and invertebrates is that invertebrates do NOT have a backbone. The first paragraph tells you that invertebrates are animals that don't have backbones. The third paragraph tells you that vertebrates have a backbone as part of their internal skeleton.

24. **(2)** The passage implies that the main difference between protozoa and metazoa is that protozoa do NOT have a fixed form. The second paragraph tells you that the bodies of protozoa have no fixed form. Then it tells you that all metazoa have fixed forms.

25. **(1)** The passage implies that the osmotic pump pill is better than other pills and capsules because it releases medicine slowly over a long period of time. The second paragraph tells you that pills and capsules dissolve too quickly. The third paragraph tells you that scientists have been trying to make a pill that can release medicine slowly over a long period of time.

26. **(2)** The way that the osmotic pump pill works is based on a process called osmosis. The forth paragraph describes a slow, steady process by which substances leave the cell. This process is identified as osmosis.

27. **(3)** The passage implies that medicine in an osmotic pump pill will leave the pill when enough pressure builds up in the pill. The last paragraph tells you that pressure builds up in the pill as water enters it. Only then is the medicine released from the pill.

28. **(1)** The passage implies that cellulose is a very porous substance because it contains millions of tiny holes. The fourth paragraph tells you that cellulose is very porous. It then goes on to say that there are millions of pores, or holes, in the cellulose walls of plants.

ANALYZING WHAT YOU READ

PART A: GENERAL READING

Read each passage. Then choose the correct answer to each question that follows the passage.

When people want hamburgers, they look for the Henny's hamburger flag. The Henny's hamburger flag is a gold bun on a field of blue. It flies at 250 restaurants nationwide. Henny's headquarters is in Paxtown. The headquarters has not just one but *two* flagpoles. The flagpoles gave Harry Gross an idea.

Gross is the chairman of Henny's, Incorporated. Gross wanted to stir up some publicity. He put an ad in the newspaper. It said, "Announcing the First Annual Flagpole Sitting Contest, sponsored by Henny's. Two contestants will battle it out in a test of will. The runner-up will receive a lifetime supply of Henny's hamburgers. The winner will receive a $100,000 home. Tell us why you should be one of the contestants." One of the contestants wrote, "I am desperate." The other wrote, "I have no choice."

The two contestants climbed their flagpoles. The top of each flagpole was surrounded by a ten-foot square platform. The contestants put their supplies on the platforms. Then they looked at each other.

"I was ready to hate the other guy," said Carl Mizzy, 25. "Then I saw that he was a she." Grace Howack, also 25, felt that same way. "I planned to dislike him. But it gets lonely up here. You got to talk to somebody, so . . . " The poles were separated by the width of the street below. Carl and Grace were close enough to talk to each other. "Not much else," says Carl.

The sitters were up for three months. By then, the press sensed romance in the air. Newspapers asked Gross to call a tie and give both of the contestants houses. Gross laughed, "They can get married and share one home."

But Carl and Grace were not ready for marriage. They each wanted their own home. Gross said he would keep to the rules. "Whoever lasts longest gets the house." Finally, after five months, the contest was over. Carl and Grace came down from their flagpoles—at the same time. "Now what is he going to do?" asked Carl. The contestants will bring the issue to court next month.

1. With which of the following statements about the contestants would Harry Gross most likely agree?

   (1) Carl and Grace did not play the contest fairly.
   (2) Carl and Grace love each other very much.
   (3) Carl and Grace should both get houses since they ended the contest at the same time.
   (4) Carl and Grace should enter the contest again next year.

2. It can be inferred from the passage that Carl and Grace are going to court because

   (1) they want to get married
   (2) Harry Gross will not give them their prizes
   (3) Harry Gross is suing them
   (4) they want to have Harry Gross arrested

3. Based on the information in the passage, you can conclude that Carl and Grace left the flagpoles at the same time because

    (1) they no longer cared about each other
    (2) they stopped caring about the contest
    (3) they thought that they both could be winners
    (4) they wanted to anger Harry Gross

Yesterday's Chester city council meeting involved a heated debate. The issue? Headphones. Councilmember Kate Matlow wants them banned. John Hanson wants to keep them. He heads SOH (Save Our Headphones).

"They're dangerous," says Matlow. "I haven't forgotten the 4th Street accident. I don't want that to happen again." Last summer, a young woman wearing headphones was crossing 4th Street. An oncoming car honked, but the woman kept on walking. She was struck and killed. "The headphones were to blame," says Matlow.

Hanson disagrees. "That woman was crossing against the light. That was a mistake in judgment. It had nothing to do with her hearing. Besides, the latest headphones do not interfere with outside noise." To prove it, Hanson wore headphones during his conversation with Matlow.

Matlow and Hanson held most of their discussion in the city hall lobby. They talked before the council meeting even started. Matlow demanded that Hanson remove his headphones. She said it was rude. Hanson said he was proving a point. "I can hear everything you say," he said.

Matlow's proposal would ban headphones from public use. "But headphones are made for public use," says Hanson. "That is the whole idea behind them. Before, people played radios in public. The sound of blasting radios was annoying. If you take away headphones, people will take out their radios again."

4. Which of the following statements is given as a fact in the passage?

    (1) People wearing headphones do not pay attention to things around them.
    (2) The sound of blasting radios annoys pedestrians.
    (3) A young woman was killed when she was wearing headphones.
    (4) The city council is going to ban headphones.

5. With which of the following statements would John Hanson most likely agree?

    (1) The extended use of headphones can cause hearing loss.
    (2) People wearing headphones pay greater attention to things.
    (3) Headphones help to block out annoying noises.
    (4) Wearing headphones doesn't increase the risk of accident.

6. Hanson implies that the woman who was killed on 4th Street was hit by the car because

    (1) she was not wearing the latest headphones
    (2) the driver ran a red light
    (3) the woman was not using her common sense
    (4) the streetlights were not working

Are children influenced by violence on TV? The Coalition for Safe Television (COST) thinks so. And they've had an effect on one of the most popular of children's cartoons—"The Seymour Squirrel Show."

Hundreds of Seymour Squirrel cartoons were made in the 50's and 60's. Rebroadcasts of the cartoons continue to be shown. COST, however, has made sure that parts of the cartoons never reach today's audience.

"Seymour Squirrel cartoons were extremely violent," says Shirley Fore, chairperson of COST. "Seymour attacked his enemy, Mr. Wolf, in the most brutal ways. In one show alone, Mr. Wolf was dropped off a cliff, blown up with TNT, and run over by a steam roller. And the violence was presented so that it was funny. We had to put a stop to this sickness."

COST put pressure on the TV stations to stop showing Seymour Squirrel cartoons. "We made the TV stations understand what kind of effect violence has on children," Fore stated. "We believe that violent shows encourage children to behave violently. They try to imitate the things that they see their heroes do. They don't understand how serious and painful violence is when it's shown to be humorous."

COST threatened to boycott any products advertised during the Seymour Squirrel shows. The TV stations reached an agreement with COST. Rather than taking Seymour Squirrel shows off the air, they agreed to cut out the violent parts.

"The shows are much better now," Fore says.

Not everyone agrees. Pete Grimes, president of the Seymour Squirrel fan club, thinks that COST has ruined the shows. "They've taken all the fun out of the cartoons. Those cartoons never hurt anyone. Kids know it's all make-believe. They're smarter than the people at COST. Kids know that there's a difference between cartoons and real life."

Psychologist Betty Freed agrees. "Violence in cartoons may actually help children deal with life. It gives them a safe outlet for their frustrations."

7. Which of the following statements from the passage is a fact?

    (1)   The original Seymour Squirrel cartoons were violent.
    (2)   The original Seymour Squirrel cartoons were funny.
    (3)   The original Seymour Squirrel cartoons helped children.
    (4)   The original Seymour Squirrel cartoons made children violent.

8. The passage implies that the TV stations cut parts of the Seymour Squirrel cartoons because

    (1)   the ratings for the cartoons were low
    (2)   the stations did not approve of violence in the shows
    (3)   COST threatened to boycott the show's sponsors
    (4)   children tried to imitate Seymour Squirrel

9. With which of the following statements would Betty Freed most likely agree?

    (1)   Children try to imitate what they see on TV.
    (2)   Children learn about violence on TV.
    (3)   Children think that cartoons present things that happen in real life.
    (4)   Cartoons do not encourage children to act violently.

Last night, artist Fred Blochard spent six hours in the Primo City jail. His crime? Painting a mural on the Mayo Textiles Company's main office building.

"It's a simple case of vandalism," says police chief Joe Russell. "Blochard was defacing private property. We have laws against that sort of thing."

A group of Blochard's supporters, who gathered outside the Mayo Building, disagree. "He wasn't damaging property, he was improving it. No one should be arrested for making our city a more interesting place to live," Marie Quinn, the spokesperson for the group, said.

Blochard has been painting for twenty years. Many of his paintings have been shown in major galleries in New York and Paris. Several have been sold for thousands of dollars. Why would he choose to paint on an office building? "I am saddened by the fact that only a small circle of rich people get to see my work. I gather the inspiration for my art from the workers. I wanted to give them something in return," Blochard said.

Richard Berry, the chairman of Mayo Textiles, is furious. "Of course I brought charges against the man. He destroyed one of the most beautiful buildings in the city. Now I'll have to spend hundreds of dollars to have the building cleaned. Blochard had better pay me back."

Blochard's supporters plan to camp out in front of the Mayo Building to prevent the removal of the mural. "Art should be part of our everyday world. It shouldn't be limited to galleries and museums," Quinn said.

The mural depicts a line of factory workers punching in at a time-clock.

10. Which of the following statements from the passage is a fact?

    (1) Blochard has to pay Berry to have the Mayo Building cleaned.
    (2) Blochard improved the Mayo Building.
    (3) Blochard was arrested for defacing private property.
    (4) Blochard should not have been arrested.

11. Blochard implies that his painting was meant to

    (1) be a gift for Marie Quinn   (2) anger factory owners
    (3) please the workers   (4) be seen by a few rich people

12. With which of the following statements would Berry most likely agree?

    (1) Blochard committed an act of vandalism.
    (2) Blochard is a very talented painter.
    (3) Blochard made a contribution to the city.
    (4) Blochard's painting belongs in a museum.

Check your answers on page 75.

PART B: PROSE LITERATURE

Read each passage. Then choose the correct answer to each question that follows the passage.

Parker's wife was sitting on the front porch floor, snapping beans. Parker was sitting on the step, some distance away, watching her sullenly. She was plain, plain. The skin on her face was thin and drawn as tight as the skin on an onion and her eyes were gray and sharp like the points of two icepicks. Parker understood why he had married her—he couldn't have got her any other way—but he couldn't understand why he stayed with her now. She was pregnant and pregnant women were not his favorite kind. Nevertheless, he stayed as if she had him conjured. He was puzzled and ashamed of himself.

The house they rented sat alone save for a single tall pecan tree on a high embankment overlooking a highway. At intervals a car would shoot past below and his wife's eyes would swerve suspiciously after the sound of it and then come back to rest on the newspaper full of beans in her lap. One of the things she did not approve of was automobiles. In addition to her other bad qualities, she was forever sniffing up sin. She did not smoke or dip, drink whiskey, use bad language or paint her face, and God knew some paint would have improved it, Parker thought. Her being against color, it was the more remarkable she had married him. Sometimes he supposed that she had married him because she meant to save him. At other times he had a suspicion that she actually liked everything she said she didn't. He could account for her one way or another; it was himself he could not understand.

1. Why was Parker ashamed of himself?

   (1) He didn't like his wife.   (2) He didn't leave his wife.
   (3) He drank too much.   (4) He used bad language too often.

2. Which of the following statements about Parker is supported by the passage?

   (1) Parker was not happy with his life.
   (2) Parker was deeply in love with his wife.
   (3) Parker was a successful businessman.
   (4) Parker did not like automobiles.

3. The tone of the passage can best be described as

   (1) happy   (2) angry   (3) passionate   (4) depressing

There are as many kinds of fences in this country as there are people. You couldn't *count* all the kinds of fences there are. There are big fences, small fences, teeny-tiny fences.

The biggest difference between one fence and another fence is whether the fence was built to protect what's inside from what's outside or to protect what's outside from what's inside. To protect the people outside, for instance, a mean dog has to be fenced in.

It's a mystery why some fences are ever built at all. Most cemeteries have fences, even though no one outside really wants to get in and no one inside ever tries to get out.

Sometimes you can't tell what a fence is keeping in — or keeping out. You can't tell what a fence is protecting from what. You suspect that sometimes people just put up fences from habit, or as a show of strength or wealth. I hate anyone who has a fence that cost more than my house cost.

The best-looking fences are often the simplest. A simple fence around a beautiful home can be like a frame around a picture. The house isn't hidden; its beauty is enhanced by the frame. But a fence can be a massive, ugly thing, too, made of bricks and mortar. Sometimes the insignificant little fences do their job just as well as the ten-foot walls. Maybe it's only a string stretched between here and there in a field. The message is clear: don't cross here.

4. The author's treatment of fences in the passage can best be described as

   (1) serious   (2) humorous   (3) factual   (4) impartial

5. With which of the following statements about fences would the author most likely agree?

   (1) The best fences are the biggest fences.
   (2) Fences don't serve any purpose.
   (3) All fences are the same.
   (4) A small fence can be as good as a big fence.

6. How does the author feel about fences that are built around cemeteries?

   (1) There is no reason to build a fence around a cemetery.
   (2) All fences that are around cemeteries are ugly.
   (3) Fences around cemeteries should be at least ten feet high.
   (4) There aren't enough fences around cemeteries.

I've quit my job with Donnegan's Plastic Box Company. Mr. Donnegan insisted that it would be better for all concerned if I left. What did I do to make them hate me so?

The first I knew of it was when Mr. Donnegan showed me the petition. Eight hundred and forty names, everyone connected with the factory, except Fanny Girden. Scanning the list quickly, I saw at once that hers was the only missing name. All the rest demanded that I be fired.

Joe Carp and Frank Reilly wouldn't talk to me about it. No one else would either, except Fanny. She was one of the few people I'd known who set her mind to something and believed it no matter what the rest of the world proved, said, or did—and Fanny did not believe that I should have been fired. She had been against the petition on principle and despite the pressure and threats she'd held out.

"Which don't mean to say," she remarked, "that I don't think there's something mighty strange about you, Charlie. Them changes. I don't know. You used to be a good, dependable, ordinary man — not too bright maybe, but honest. Who knows what you done to yourself to get so smart all of a sudden. Like everybody around here's been saying, Charlie, it's not right."

7. The passage implies that the narrator quit his job at the box company because

   (1) he didn't like the job
   (2) he felt he was too smart for the job
   (3) almost everyone at the factory wanted him to be fired
   (4) Joe Carp and Frank Reilly wouldn't talk to him

8. Which of the following words best describes the way that the narrator feels about the petition?

   (1) puzzled   (2) angered   (3) annoyed   (4) frightened

9. From the information in the passage, you can conclude that the narrator was **not** liked at the box company because he had

   (1) become smart   (2) fought with the other workers
   (3) worked too hard   (4) threatened Fanny Girden

I know what is being said about me and you can take my side or theirs, that's your own business. It's my word against Eunice's and Olivia-Ann's, and it should be plain enough to anyone with two good eyes which one of us has their wits about them. I just want the citizens of the U.S.A. to know the facts, that's all.

The facts: On Sunday, August 12, this year of our Lord, Eunice tried to kill me with her papa's Civil War sword and Olivia-Ann cut up all over the place with a fourteen-inch hog knife. This is not even to mention lots of other things.

It began six months ago when I married Marge. That was the first thing I did wrong. We were married in Mobile after an acquaintance of only four days. We were both sixteen and she was visiting my cousin Georgia. Now that I've had plenty of time to think it over, I can't for the life of me figure how I fell for the likes of her. She has no looks, no body, and no brains whatsoever. But Marge is a natural blonde and maybe that's the answer. Well, we were married going on three months when Marge ups and gets pregnant; the second thing I did wrong. Then she starts hollering that she's got to go home to Mama — only she hasn't got no mama, just these two aunts, Eunice and Olivia-Ann. So she makes me quit my perfectly swell position clerking at the Cash'n' Carry and move here to Admiral's Mill which is nothing but a damn gap in the road any way you care to consider it.

10. The narrator blames his problems with Eunice and Olivia-Ann on

   (1) his job   (2) his marriage
   (3) his cousin Georgia   (4) his wife's mother

11. Which of the following words best describes the narrator's feelings toward Admiral's Mill?

   (1) fear   (2) awe   (3) envy   (4) disgust

12. Which of the following words best describes the way in which the narrator presents the information in the passage?

   (1) slanted   (2) factual   (3) puzzled   (4) unconcerned

Check your answers on page 76.

PART C: SOCIAL STUDIES

Read each passage. Then choose the correct answer to each question that follows the passage.

Ambex Oil Company feels you should know the facts. Congress wants to put a twelve dollar fee on each barrel of imported oil. Congress says that the fees are good for you. Don't bet on it!

THEY SAY: The import fee will make oil more expensive for Americans. Americans will buy less oil. Foreign oil producers will lower their prices to encourage Americans to buy. Oil will cost less than ever before.

WE SAY: None of this is true! First, Americans will not buy less oil. We Americans have tightened our belts already. We've built energy-saving factories. We're driving our cars as little as possible. Our thermostats are set as low as possible.

We don't think that oil prices will be reduced. Foreign oil producers supply the world with millions of barrels of oil daily. The bold sacrifices of Americans would not affect them. The sacrifices would put only a tiny dent in their market.

THEY SAY: The import fee will change domestic oil prices. Domestic oil producers will raise the price of their oil to equal the price of imported oil. Domestic producers will like these new, higher prices. They will drill for more domestic oil to sell. America will have more domestic oil than ever before.

WE SAY: The price of domestic oil will go up. But domestic producers will not drill for more oil. No one is sure how much oil is under our land. Domestic producers will not risk millions of dollars drilling for oil.

Meanwhile, Americans will share the burden of the import fee. Oil companies will be forced to raise oil prices to offset the fee. We may have to raise the price of oil 25¢ a gallon. Of course, this would be a near disaster for the economy. We would see a rise in unemployment and inflation.

Tell Congress you don't want to pay 25¢ more a gallon. Tell Congress you don't want a weak economy. Tell Congress the import fee is a very, very bad bet.

1. The author of this passage is most likely a representative of

   (1) Ambex Oil Company   (2) Congress
   (3) the American public   (4) foreign oil producers

2. With which of the following statements about the fees on imported oil would the author most likely agree?

   (1) The fees will help Americans to conserve energy.
   (2) The fees will make more oil available to Americans.
   (3) The fees will lead to an increase in inflation.
   (4) The fees will make the American economy stronger.

3. You can conclude that the main purpose of this passage is to get Americans to

   (1) pay 25¢ a gallon more for oil
   (2) oppose the fees on imported oil
   (3) use less oil than ever before
   (4) avoid using oil produced in foreign countries

Freedom of the press is a basic American freedom. It is protected by the First Amendment to the Constitution.

Very few people would argue against giving freedom to the press. That's because, for the most part, the press does a good job. Newspapers, magazines, and broadcasters are basically responsible. They don't abuse their rights.

But once in a while somebody causes trouble. Somebody causes people to think that maybe the press should have limits on its freedom. Dewey Belcher is such a person.

Dewey Belcher calls himself a magazine publisher. What he publishes is a 12-page newspaper. The newspaper is appropriately called "Slime Time." The newspaper is filled with pictures of naked men and women. But these are not your normal nudie pictures. The people who are in the pictures all look like famous movie and TV stars. But none of the people are really famous. They're all look-alikes of famous stars.

Belcher prints the pictures of these look-alikes. But he doesn't identify the people as look-alikes. Instead, he leads his readers to believe that the pictures are actual portraits of famous people.

Three months ago, Belcher printed a nude picture of a woman who looked like actress FiFi LaJoy. Ms. LaJoy heard about the picture. She decided to sue Belcher for $4 million. Belcher is defending himself on the grounds that he has the right to print whatever he wants. His right, he feels, is protected by the First Amendment.

"Belcher is a menace," said Garrett V. Burns, head of the Society of American Publishers. "He's a menace because he can really make things bad for us. We publishers work hard. We don't take our freedom for granted. We know that anything can happen. Somebody like Belcher can turn people against us. He can make it that much harder for us to do our jobs."

Despite Belcher's obvious abuses, he has some supporters. He is being defended by the National Liberty Group. The NLG is a society of lawyers. Its purpose is to protect the rights of anyone who asks for protection.

"We don't like what Belcher publishes," said Malcolm Wert of the NLG. "But we'll defend his right to publish it."

4. Which of the following statements about Dewey Belcher is NOT a fact from the passage?

   (1) Dewey Belcher is a menace.
   (2) Dewey Belcher publishes a 12-page newspaper.
   (3) Dewey Belcher is being sued for $4 million.
   (4) Dewey Belcher is being defended by the National Liberty Group.

5. From the passage, you can infer that Garrett V. Burns thinks that Dewey Belcher is a menace because he is afraid that

   (1) people will believe the pictures that Belcher prints
   (2) Belcher's newspaper will become too popular
   (3) the press will lose some of its rights because of Belcher
   (4) Belcher will put a picture of Burns in his next newspaper

6. Which of the following words best describes the author's feelings toward Dewey Belcher?

   (1) disgust   (2) admiration   (3) fear   (4) satisfaction

In Pauxet County Prison, a man named John Reddy is behind bars. He committed a murder. But is he guilty?

John is twenty years old. Last year, he planned to rob a gas station. He brought a gun with him. "I was going to wave it at the attendant," says John. "Then he would do what I say." But when the attendant went to the cash register, he did not take out money. He took out a gun. "I panicked," says John. "I pulled the trigger." John thinks a moment. "What else could I do?"

John is the son of child abusers. The neighbors suspected the slaps and beatings, but did nothing. "When Johnny came to school with bruises, I worried," says a teacher. "I meant to call his parents. But I was afraid of what might happen. I didn't want to get involved." When John was ten, his father left home. The beatings stopped. His mother started drinking heavily. But she left John alone.

He cut classes in junior high. He hung out with neighborhood kids. He used drugs. "Everybody did," says John. His friends dared each other to do things. "That's how you belonged." Two friends dared John to steal something. They walked into a store with him. John picked up a radio. He put it under his jacket. Then he felt a hand on his shoulder. It was a store detective. And John's friends were nowhere in sight.

John was sent to a juvenile detention center. He was there two months. He was surrounded by con artists and thieves. "I learned a lot from them," says John.

John wanted money, and he wanted to work for it. He was a night watchman at a factory for a while. Then they heard about his record. He was fired. John went to a job-placement office. The clerks were white. " 'What are your skills?' they asked. I told them I got my hands. I could work a machine. I could drive a truck. They said they didn't have anything. When I was walking out I overheard something. A white man was saying he didn't have a high school diploma. The clerk was saying it was no problem."

John slipped in and out of odd jobs. Then a friend gave him heroin. "I thought I was smart enough. No way I could be a junkie." But John got hooked. The day he walked into the gas station, his hands were shaking. "I needed, you know . . ." His voice fades. "I am so tired," he says. "I am so tired."

7. The author's attitude toward John Reddy can best be described as

    (1) understanding   (2) uncaring   (3) hostile   (4) removed

8. The passage implies that John Reddy could not get a job from the job-placement office because of his

    (1) lack of education   (2) criminal record
    (3) color   (4) addiction to drugs

9. With which of the following statements about John Reddy would the author most likely agree?

    (1) John Reddy deserves to be in jail.
    (2) John Reddy is hopelessly addicted to drugs.
    (3) John Reddy is not completely responsible for his crimes.
    (4) John Reddy's main problem was that he could not keep a job.

Address myself to Vietnam for two minutes? It's a shame — that's one second. It is, it's a shame. You put the government on the spot when you even mention Vietnam. They feel embarrassed — you notice that? They wish they would not even have to read the newspapers about South Vietnam, and you can't blame them. It's just a trap that they let themselves get into. It's John Foster Dulles they're trying to blame it on, because he's dead.

But they're trapped, they can't get out. You notice I said "they." *They* are trapped, *they* can't get out. If they pour more men in, they'll get deeper. If they pull the men out, it's a defeat. And they should have known it in the first place.

France had about 200,000 Frenchmen over there, and the most highly mechanized modern army sitting on this earth. And those little rice farmers ate them up, and their tanks, and everything else. Yes, they did, and France was deeply entrenched, had been there a hundred or more years. Now, if she couldn't stay there and was entrenched, why, you are out of your mind if you think Sam can get in over there.

But we're not supposed to say that. If we say that, we're anti-American, or we're seditious, or we're subversive, or we're advocating something that's not intelligent. So that's two minutes, sir.

10. In the passage, the word "they" refers to

    (1) South Vietnam   (2) the French government
    (3) the American government (4) the French army

11. Based on the passage, you can conclude that the author blamed the problems in Vietnam on

    (1) South Vietnam   (2) John Foster Dulles
    (3) France   (4) the American government

12. With which of the following statements about Vietnam would the author have agreed based on the passage?

    (1) People who opposed the war in Vietnam were anti-American.
    (2) The American government made a mistake by getting involved in Vietnam.
    (3) America had a much better chance than France to win a war in Vietnam.
    (4) It was the duty of the American government to send troops to Vietnam.

Check your answers on page 77.

PART D: SCIENCE

Read each passage. Then choose the correct answer to each question that follows the passage.

Caffeine is a chemical that can be found naturally in coffee, tea, kola nuts, and cocoa. Caffeine can also be made in a laboratory, and the chemical is often added to soft drinks and medicines. Tests have proved that caffeine affects the body by increasing the heart rate and rhythm, which in turn affects the circulatory system. Caffeine also stimulates the secretion of acids in the stomach, and it increases urination.

In 1972, a team of scientists issued a report on the health problems associated with caffeine. These scientists linked heavy caffeine use with heart disease. They suggested that people should limit their caffeine intake.

Recently, Dr. B. K. Smerl disputed the 1972 report on caffeine. The doctor stated in a medical journal that he had spent four years studying caffeine. He claimed that his study proved that caffeine could not be linked with heart disease. He said that caffeine is actually good for the body because it stimulates the system. Caffeine, the doctor claimed, makes the body operate more effectively.

Several doctors commented on this study to the press. "It's difficult to take this report seriously," Dr. Wilson, of Hooker Medical School, stated. "The study was funded by a company that uses caffeine in its products. I won't believe this report until the study is also conducted by a more impartial researcher."

1. Which of the following statements from the passage is an opinion?

   (1) People should limit their caffeine intake.
   (2) Caffeine speeds up the heart rate.
   (3) Caffeine stimulates the secretion of stomach acids.
   (4) Caffeine was linked to heart disease in a 1972 study.

2. With which of the following statements would Dr. Wilson most likely agree?

   (1) Dr. Smerl's study on caffeine was conducted in an impartial, scientific manner.
   (2) Dr. Smerl's study was fixed to show that caffeine isn't harmful.
   (3) Another study will confirm that caffeine is good for the body.
   (4) Additional research on caffeine was not necessary after the 1972 study.

3. Which of the following statements from the passage is a fact?

   (1) Caffeine does not cause heart disease.
   (2) Dr. Smerl's study did not prove that caffeine can be linked to heart disease.
   (3) Dr. Smerl's study was based on unreliable data.
   (4) People have been consuming too much caffeine.

Can some people move objects with the power of their mind? Can they read other people's thoughts? Do some people have special psychic powers? For years, magicians have spellbound audiences with tricks that make the magicians seem psychic. But recently, some magicians have been playing for a special audience. They have been playing tricks on scientists.

A group of scientists at Wheatley University in Goldenrod, Wyoming, were trying to see if some people actually do have psychic powers. A famous magician, Omar the Mystic, sent two of his best students to the university. The young magicians told the scientists that they were psychics.

Over a two-year period, the teenaged magicians spent over 200 hours participating in university experiments. The scientists never suspected that their star subjects were fakes. "These two kids are the real thing. I think we've proven that the mind has incredible powers," the head of the research team reported.

In one demonstration of their powers, the boys bent metal objects simply by touching them. Actually, the boys distracted the scientists and bent the wires when the scientists weren't looking. In another trick, the boys made a chair move across the room with their mental powers. They really moved the chair with a piece of fine wire. And in another display of their psychic powers, the boys guessed which cards the scientists were holding. The magicians had only performed a simple card trick.

Just before the scientists were about to publish the results of their study, Omar revealed his trick to the press. "I was simply conducting my own experiment," Omar claimed. "Scientists want to believe in the supernatural. They're more careless when it comes to testing subjects who say they're psychic. It's not that I don't believe that some people have special powers. I'm all for study in this field of psychology. But if scientists don't become more scientific, they may never be able to gather reliable data about psychics."

"These magicians have wasted our time and money," the scientists at Wheatley University commented. "They lied to us and ruined our experiment. And they've hardly helped to improve studies on psychics. Now it will be nearly impossible for anyone to take research on psychics seriously."

4. You can infer from the passage that Omar the Mystic sent his two students to the university to

    (1) help the scientists
    (2) trick the scientists
    (3) prove that psychics exist
    (4) prove that he was a great magician

5. The scientists' reaction to what Omar did can best be described as

    (1) forgiving   (2) embarrassed   (3) angry   (4) grateful

6. With which of the following statements about psychic powers would Omar the Mystic most likely agree?

    (1) There are no people that have psychic powers.
    (2) Only magicians have psychic powers.
    (3) Only Omar the Mystic has psychic powers.
    (4) Some people probably have psychic powers.

In children's fairy tale books, the wicked witch is usually pictured with several large warts on her chin. Everyone agrees that warts are unattractive. And anyone who gets a wart wants it to go away immediately. But drugstore shelves are lined with wart-removal products that don't always work. Even when doctors treat warts by burning, freezing, or drying them out of the skin, there's no guarantee that they'll leave.

Some doctors have been experimenting with hypnosis as a treatment for warts. One doctor says that he has proven that hypnosis can remove warts. "I put my patients in a hypnotic trance. Then I tell them that their warts will disappear. It's worked with all of my patients. Their warts were gone in several months. I believe that their warts disappeared because of this treatment." The doctor has treated twelve patients with this method.

"I think the hypnosis really worked," said Skip Hopkins, one of the doctor's patients. "I was taking a wart-removal medicine before I went to the doctor. It didn't get rid of the wart. Then a few weeks after I had hypnosis, the wart disappeared."

The truth of the matter is that only time and the human body can cure warts. Doctors have yet to come up with a cure that works all the time. Common warts are caused by viruses. When a virus infects the top layer of the skin, it causes abnormal cells to grow. From its "base" on the top layer, the wart travels under the skin. All warts, however, will disappear over time even if they're not treated. As long as the body is healthy, the wart will mysteriously disappear eventually. The amount of time it takes for this to happen ranges from a few weeks to a few years.

7. Which of the following statements about the information in the passage is an opinion?

   (1) Hypnosis is being used as a treatment for warts.
   (2) Skip Hopkin's wart disappeared because of hypnosis.
   (3) Doctors can treat warts by drying them out of the skin.
   (4) The patients' warts disappeared after they had hypnosis.

8. With which of the following statements about warts would the author of the passage most likely agree?

   (1) There isn't enough proof that hypnosis cures warts.
   (2) Only hypnosis can cure warts.
   (3) No one knows what causes warts.
   (4) Using wart-removal medicine is the best way to treat warts.

9. The author of the passage thinks that Skip Hopkins's wart disappeared because of

   (1) hypnosis   (2) wart-removal medicine
   (3) normal body functions   (4) an infection from a virus

Check your answers on page 78.

ANSWERS AND EXPLANATIONS

Part A: General Reading

1. **(1)** Harry Gross would most likely agree that Carl and Grace did not play the contest fairly. The second paragraph tells you that, according to the contest rules, the runner-up would receive hamburgers and the winner would receive a home. Gross would most likely agree that when Carl and Grace ended the game in a tie they were not playing fair.

2. **(2)** You can infer from the passage that Carl and Grace are going to court because Harry Gross will not give them their prizes. In paragraph 5, Gross refused to call a tie and said that the contestants should share one home. You can infer that Carl and Grace are bringing Gross to court because he will not give each of them a home.

3. **(3)** You can conclude that Carl and Grace left the flagpoles at the same time because they thought they both could be winners. The last paragraph tells you that they both wanted to receive first prize. They came down the flagpoles at the same time so that they both could be winners.

4. **(3)** The statement that a young woman was killed when she was wearing headphones is a fact. Paragraph 2 tells you that a woman was killed on 4th Street when she was wearing headphones.

5. **(4)** John Hanson would most likely agree with the statement that wearing headphones doesn't increase the risk of accident. In paragraph 3, Hanson says that the woman's accident was not due to the headphones. He says that the woman's accident was not related to her hearing.

6. **(3)** Hanson implies that the woman was hit by the car because she was not using her common sense. In paragraph 3, Hanson says the woman made a mistake in judgment. He says the accident had nothing to do with her hearing.

7. **(1)** The statement that the original Seymour Squirrel cartoons were violent is a fact. Paragraph 3 tells you that one cartoon character was dropped off a cliff and blown up with TNT. All of the people quoted in the passage agree that there was violence in the cartoons.

8. **(3)** The passage implies that the TV stations cut parts of the Seymour Squirrel cartoons because COST threatened to boycott the show's sponsors. Paragraph 5 tells you that COST threatened to boycott any products advertised during the show.

9. **(4)** Betty Freed would most likely agree with the statement that cartoons do not encourage children to act violently. In the last paragraph, Freed says that the cartoons give children a safe outlet for their frustrations. The word "safe" clues you that Freed does not think that cartoons make children act violently.

10. **(3)** The statement that Blochard was arrested for defacing private property is a fact. The first paragraph tells you that Blochard spent six hours in jail. The second paragraph tells you that he was arrested for defacing private property.

11. **(3)** Blochard implies that his painting was meant to please the workers. In paragraph 4, Blochard says that workers are the inspiration for his art, and that he wanted to give them something in return. His mural was meant as a present for the workers.

12. **(1)** Berry would most likely agree with the statement that Blochard committed an act of vandalism. In paragraph 5, Berry says that Blochard destroyed one of the most beautiful buildings in the city. Destroying a building is an act of vandalism.

Part B: Prose Literature

1. **(2)** Parker was ashamed of himself because he didn't leave his wife. The first paragraph tells you that Parker couldn't understand why he stayed with his wife. He stayed with her as if she had him "conjured," or tricked by magic. You can infer that he was ashamed of himself for not leaving her.

2. **(1)** The statement that Parker was not happy with his life is supported by the passage. The first paragraph tells you that Parker was puzzled and ashamed of himself. The second paragraph tells you that he couldn't understand himself. You can infer that Parker was unhappy with himself and his life.

3. **(4)** The tone of the passage can best be described as depressing. Parker is unhappy with his life, but he doesn't try to change it. He broods about how miserable he feels.

4. **(2)** The author's treatment of fences can best be described as humorous. In paragraphs 3 and 4, the author points out how silly some fences are. The jokes in these paragraphs give the passage a humorous tone.

5. **(4)** The author would most likely agree with the statement that a small fence can be as good as a big fence. In paragraph 5, the author tells you that sometimes little fences do their job as well as ten-foot walls.

6. **(1)** The author feels that there is no reason to build a fence around a cemetery. In paragraph 3, the author tells you that no one outside really wants to get into a cemetery, and no one inside ever tries to get out.

7. **(3)** The narrator quit his job at the box company because almost everyone at the factory wanted him to be fired. In the second paragraph, the narrator tells you that 840 people signed a petition asking him to be fired. You can infer that the author had to either quit or be fired.

8. **(1)** The word "puzzled" best describes the way that the narrator felt about the petition. In the first paragraph, the narrator asks, "What did I do to make them hate me so?" He doesn't understand why they signed the petition.

9. **(1)** You can conclude that the narrator was not liked at the box company because he had become smart. In the last paragraph, Fanny Girden tells the narrator that he had become smart all of a sudden, and that it was not right.

10. **(2)** The narrator blames his problems with Eunice and Olivia-Ann on his marriage. In paragraph 3, the narrator says that the problem began six months ago when he married Marge. Then he describes how his wife forced him to live with Eunice and Olivia-Ann.

11. **(4)** The word "disgust" best describes the narrator's feelings toward Admiral's Mill. In paragraph 3, the narrator describes Admiral's Mill as nothing but a gap in the road.

12. **(1)** The word "slanted" best describes the way in which the narrator presents the information in the passage. In the first paragraph, the narrator tells you that the story is his word against his aunts'. In the second paragraph, the narrator tells you he is giving you the facts, but you can infer that his opinion is slanted.

Part C: Social Studies

1. **(1)** The author of this passage is most likely a representative of Ambex Oil Company. In paragraph 1, Ambex Oil Company is identified as the one giving the facts. The passage tries to persuade you to be against fees on imported oil.

2. **(3)** The author would most likely agree with the statement that fees on imported oil will lead to an increase in inflation. The next-to-last paragraph tells you that the fees would mean a rise in inflation.

3. **(2)** The main purpose of this passage is to get Americans to oppose the fees on imported oil. In the last paragraph, Ambex Oil Company asks you to tell Congress to vote against the import fee.

4. **(1)** The statement that Dewey Belcher is a menace is NOT a fact. The statement is an opinion.

5. **(3)** You can infer that Garrett V. Burns thinks that Dewey Belcher is a menace because he is afraid that the press will lose some of its rights because of Belcher. In paragraph 7, Garrett Burns says that he and other publishers don't take freedom of the press for granted. Garrett says that Belcher may turn people against the press.

6. **(1)** "Disgust" is the word that best describes the author's feelings toward Dewey Belcher. In paragraph 4, the author tells you that Belcher's newspaper is appropriately called "Slime Time." In paragraph 8, the author remarks that "despite Belcher's obvious abuses," he has some supporters. You can infer that the author disapproves of Belcher.

7. **(1)** The author's attitude toward John Reddy can best be described as understanding. The author looks for reasons for Reddy's actions. The author points out that Reddy comes from a family of child abusers and had bad friends. The author tries to understand why Reddy committed the crime.

8. **(3)** The passage implies that John Reddy could not get a job from the job-placement office because of his color. In paragraph 6, Reddy tells you that the placement office told him that it didn't have any jobs for unskilled workers. Reddy goes on to say that an unskilled white man was told that there were jobs available. You can conclude that Reddy is not white, and that he was denied a job because of his color.

9. **(3)** The author would most likely agree with the statement that John Reddy is not completely responsible for his crimes. In the first paragraph, the author asks if Reddy is really guilty. The author describes the problems of Reddy's life. The author tries to convince you that Reddy's problems make him not completely responsible for his crimes.

10. **(3)** In the passage, the word "they" refers to the American government. In the first paragraph, the author says you put the government on the spot when you mention Vietnam. In the last paragraph, the author says we are not supposed to embarrass the government because it makes us anti-American. These clues tell you that "they" is the American government.

11. **(4)** You can conclude that the author blamed the problems in Vietnam on the American government. In the first paragraph, the author says that Vietnam is a trap that the American government let itself get into.

12. **(2)** The author would have agreed with the statement that the American government made a mistake by getting involved in Vietnam. In the first paragraph, the author calls the Vietnam involvement a shame. In the second paragraph, he says that America is trapped and can't get out.

Part D: Science

1. **(1)** The statement that people should limit their caffeine intake is an opinion. Paragraph 2 tells you that scientists "suggested" that caffeine intake should be limited based on their study. The word "suggested" tells you that this is not a fact.

2. **(2)** Dr. Wilson would most likely agree with the statement that Dr. Smerl's study was fixed to show that caffeine isn't harmful. In the last paragraph, Dr. Wilson says that he doesn't take Dr. Smerl's study seriously. He implies that the study was fixed when he says that Dr. Smerl's study was funded by a company that uses caffeine in its products.

3. **(2)** The statement that Dr. Smerl's study did not prove that caffeine can be linked to heart disease is a fact. Dr. Smerl's study (paragraph 3) tried to show that caffeine *can't* be linked to heart disease.

4. **(2)** You can infer that Omar the Mystic sent his students to the university in order to trick the scientists. The first paragraph tells you that some magicians have been playing tricks on scientists. The passage goes on to describe how Omar played a trick on scientists at Wheatley University.

5. **(3)** The scientists' reaction to what Omar did can best be described as angry. In the last paragraph, the scientists say the magicians have wasted their time and money. The scientists add that now it will be hard for psychic research to be taken seriously. You can infer that the scientists are angry.

6. **(4)** Omar the Mystic would most likely agree with the statement that some people probably have psychic powers. In paragraph 5, Omar says that he is all for the study of psychics.

7. **(2)** The statement that Skip Hopkins's wart disappeared because of hypnosis is an opinion. Skip Hopkins thinks that hypnosis caused his wart to go away; however, this is not a fact. The passage gives other reasons why the wart could have disappeared. Paragraph 3 tells you that Hopkins was using wart-removal medicine. Paragraph 4 tells you that warts will disappear even if they're not treated.

8. **(1)** The author would agree with the statement that there isn't enough proof that hypnosis cures warts. In the last paragraph, the author tells you that a wart will disappear eventually all by itself. There is no proof that Skip Hopkins's wart disappeared because of hypnosis.

9. **(3)** The author of the passage thinks that Skip Hopkins's wart disappeared because of normal body functions. In the last paragraph, the author says that the truth is that only time and the human body can cure warts.

READING TABLES, GRAPHS, AND DIAGRAMS

PART A: GENERAL READING

Use the illustrations to answer the questions.

FOOD VALUES OF SIX FOODS

Food	Serving Size	Calories	Protein (in grams)	Fat (in grams)	Carbohydrates (in grams)
ground beef	3 ounces	185	23	10	0
tuna (drained)	3 ounces	120	24	7	0
cream-style corn	1 cup	210	5	2	51
green beans	1 cup	35	2	0	8
apple	1	80	0	1	20
coffeecake	1 slice	230	5	7	38

1. According to the chart, how many grams of protein are in one cup of cream-style corn?

   (1) 0   (2) 2   (3) 5   (4) 24

2. According to the chart, how many grams of carbohydrates are in a single apple?

   (1) 8   (2) 20   (3) 38   (4) 51

3. According to the chart, which food has no grams of fat in a serving?

   (1) tuna   (2) coffeecake   (3) apple   (4) green beans

4. If a dieter wanted a low-calorie main course, which of the following foods from the chart would be the BEST choice for the main course?

   (1) drained tuna   (2) ground beef
   (3) coffeecake   (4) cream-style corn

**Hours and Usage of Public Buses West City
(Monday through Friday)**

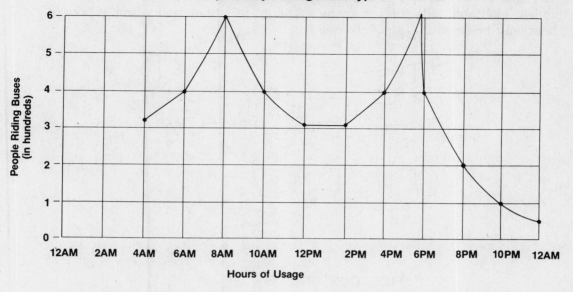

Hours of Usage

5. According to the graph, about how many people ride West City public buses at 6 AM?

(1) 300   (2) 400   (3) 500   (4) 600

6. According to the graph, about how many people ride West City public buses at 8 PM?

(1) 100   (2) 200   (3) 300   (4) 400

7. From the information in the graph, you can infer that there are no public buses running in the city between

(1) 12 AM and 4 AM   (2) 6 AM and 12 PM
(3) 2 AM and 8 AM   (4) 12 PM and 6 PM

8. Suppose the West City Council decided to add buses at the hours of highest usage. At what times would the buses be added?

(1) 12 AM and 12 PM   (2) 8 AM and 5 PM
(3) 8 AM and 8 PM   (4) 12 AM and 5 PM

What is the cheapest fuel that you can use to heat your home? The chart and map below can help to answer this question. The map is divided into five zones. The table tells you the average amount of money that it would take to heat your home with each of the five fuels.

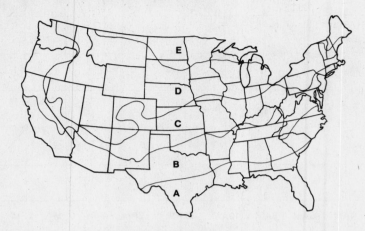

FUEL COST TABLE

Type of Fuel	Zone				
	A	B	C	D	E
Oil	$325	$700	$950	$1,125	$1,325
Gas	$250	$515	$575	$760	$985
Electricity	$475	$1,065	$1,465	$1,755	$2,050
Coal	$250	$390	$520	$615	$715
Wood	$225	$420	$595	$695	$805

9. According to the table, how much would it cost a person living in Zone C to heat his home with coal?

    (1) $390   (2) $520   (3) $575   (4) $595

10. A person who lives in Zone B changes from oil heat to gas heat. How much money can that person expect to save on fuel, according to the table?

    (1) $185   (2) $265   (3) $515   (4) $700

11. According to the table, how much would it cost a person living in Zone D to heat his home with gas?

    (1) $575   (2) $615   (3) $760   (4) $985

12. Which of the following statements about heating fuel costs can be inferred from the table?

    (1) Wood is the cheapest fuel to use in all five zones.
    (2) Electricity is the most expensive fuel to use in all five zones.
    (3) Coal is the cheapest fuel to use in all five zones.
    (4) Oil is the most expensive fuel to use in all five zones.

Some people don't believe that driving more slowly can save lives. But the truth of the matter is that driving more slowly can help a person to avoid serious accidents.

The following illustration shows the distance that it takes to stop a car at a given speed. The distance is measured in feet. The shaded area shows the driver's thinking distance. That's the distance that it takes the driver to react to a danger that he sees. The white area shows the vehicle's braking distance. That's the distance that it takes for the car to stop once the brakes are applied. The number at the top of each bar shows the total number of feet that it takes to stop the car.

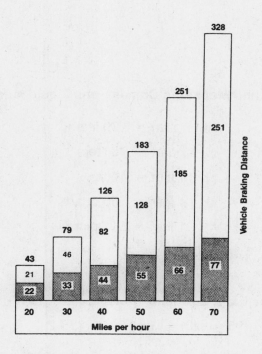

13. According to the illustration, what is the total number of feet needed to stop a car that is traveling at 50 miles per hour?

    (1) 55   (2) 126   (3) 128   (4) 183

14. According to the illustration, what is the vehicle braking distance for a car that is traveling at 60 miles per hour?

    (1) 66 feet   (2) 128 feet   (3) 185 feet   (4) 251 feet

15. Which of the following statements about the driver's thinking distance is supported by the illustration?

    (1) The driver's thinking distance increases as the speed of the car increases.
    (2) People who drive faster do not think as quickly as people who drive more slowly.
    (3) The driver's thinking distance is more important than the vehicle braking distance.
    (4) People who think fast are able to reduce the vehicle braking distance.

16. Which of the following statements about braking and speed is supported by the illustration?

    (1) A driver with good reflexes can stop his car quickly at any speed.
    (2) The speed of a vehicle has a direct effect on the distance needed to stop the vehicle.
    (3) The vehicle braking distance increases only when a person drives faster than 50 miles per hour.
    (4) The relation between the speed of a vehicle and the total distance needed to stop the vehicle is not important.

Weights and Measures Conversions (liquid measure)

1 gallon = 3.79 liters

1 quart = .95 liters

1 pint = .47 liters

1 liter = 1.06 quarts

1 liter = 2.11 pints

1,000 liters = 1 kiloliter

17. According to the table, how many pints are in 1 liter?

    (1) .47   (2) .95   (3) 1.06   (4) 2.11

18. According to the table, how many liters are in 1 gallon?

    (1) 1.06   (2) 2.11   (3) 3.79   (4) 1,000

19. According to the table, you can infer that 2 quarts is equal to

    (1) exactly 2 liters   (2) a little less than 2 liters
    (3) a little more than 2 liters   (4) half of 1 liter

20. What would you conclude is the largest unit of measurement listed in the table?

    (1) liter   (2) quart   (3) gallon   (4) kiloliter

Check your answers on page 98.

PART B: SOCIAL STUDIES

Use the illustrations to answer the questions.

Gross National Products and Per Capita Incomes for 5 Nations

Nation	Gross National Product (in billions)		Per Capita Income	
Brazil	$214.58	(1979)	$1,523	(1978)
Japan	$990	(1980)	$8,460	(1980)
Nigeria	$43	(1978)	$523	(1978)
Norway	$57.32	(1980)	$7,949	(1978)
U.S.A.	$2,576.6	(1980)	$8,612	(1978)

The gross national product is the value of all goods and services that a nation produces. The per capita income is the average earned income for a citizen of that nation.

1. According to the table, what was the gross national product for Japan in 1980?

   (1) $990   (2) $990,000   (3) $990 million   (4) $990 billion

2. According to the table, which nation had a per capita income of $7,949 in 1978?

   (1) Brazil   (2) Nigeria   (3) Norway   (4) U.S.A.

3. Which of the nations listed in the table had the highest gross national product of all the nations in the table?

   (1) Brazil   (2) Japan   (3) Norway   (4) U.S.A.

4. According to the table, the average person in Nigeria in 1978 earned

   (1) no income   (2) less than $1,000
   (3) exactly $1,000   (4) more than $1,000

Age Distribution of Americans

Under 5 years	5-19	20-44	45-64	65 and over
1830				
1880				
1930				
1980				

Each figure = about 6% of U.S. population

5. According to the graph, in which of the following years were there the most children under 5 years of age?

   (1) 1830   (2) 1880   (3) 1930   (4) 1980

6. According to the graph, what percent of the U.S. population was between 45 and 64 years old in 1980?

   (1) 6%   (2) 12%   (3) 24%   (4) 32%

7. According to the graph, which of the following age groups in 1930 was the largest?

   (1) under 5   (2) 5–19   (3) 20–44   (4) 45–64

8. According to the graph, you can conclude that the trend of the U.S. population on a whole is to have

   (1) more children and to live longer
   (2) fewer children and to live shorter
   (3) more children and to live shorter
   (4) fewer children and to live longer

Households in Mannix County Over the Last Ten Years

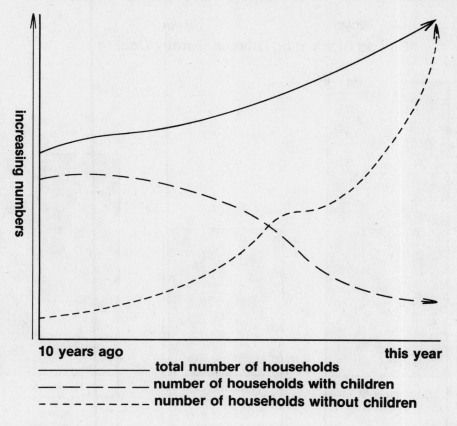

_____ total number of households

— — — — — number of households with children

— — — — — — — — number of households without children

9. From information in the graph, you can infer that over the last 10 years the number of all households in Mannix County has

   (1) decreased greatly   (2) decreased slightly
   (3) increased slightly   (4) remained the same

10. From information in the graph, you can infer that over the last 10 years the number of households without children in Mannix County has

   (1) increased greatly   (2) decreased greatly
   (3) remained the same   (4) decreased slightly

11. From information in the graph, you can infer that over the last 10 years the number of households with children in Mannix County has

   (1) increased greatly   (2) increased slightly
   (3) decreased greatly   (4) remained the same

12. From information in the graph, which of the following will most likely be true about households in Mannix County in the near future?

   (1) The number of households without children will increase.
   (2) The number of all households will decrease.
   (3) The number of households with children will increase.
   (4) The number of households without children will remain the same.

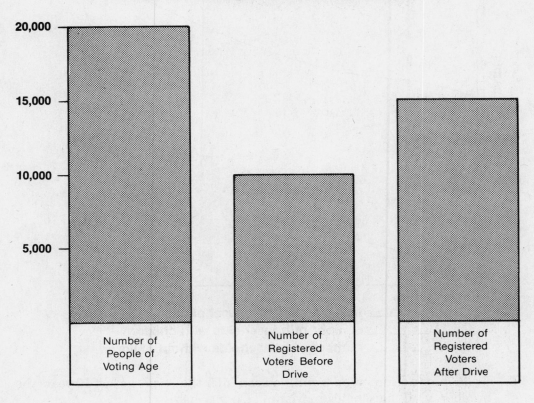

Effects of a Voting Drive in Gurney County

13. According to the graph, how many people of voting age are in Gurney County?

    (1) 5,000   (2) 10,000   (3) 10,500   (4) 20,000

14. According to the graph, how many people were registered voters before the voting drive?

    (1) 5,000   (2) 10,000   (3) 10,500   (4) 20,000

15. According to the graph, how many people were registered voters after the voting drive?

    (1) 5,000   (2) 10,000   (3) 15,000   (4) 20,000

16. From information in the graph, you can conclude that the voting drive in Gurney County had

    (1) no effect on the number of registered voters
    (2) increased the total number of people of voting age
    (3) decreased the number of registered voters
    (4) increased the number of registered voters

How Marvin City Spends a Resident's Tax Dollar

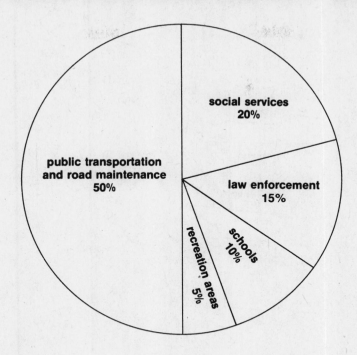

17. According to the graph, what percent of a Marvin City resident's tax dollar is spent on law enforcement?

    (1) 5%   (2) 10%   (3) 15%   (4) 20%

18. According to the graph, what percent of a Marvin City resident's tax dollar is spent on social services?

    (1) 20%   (2) 15%   (3) 10%   (4) 5%

19. According to the graph, which program receives the least money from a Marvin City resident's tax dollar?

    (1) public transportation and road maintenance
    (2) law enforcement
    (3) schools
    (4) recreation areas

20. Which program uses half of a Marvin City resident's tax dollar?

    (1) public transportation and road maintenance
    (2) social services
    (3) law enforcement
    (4) schools

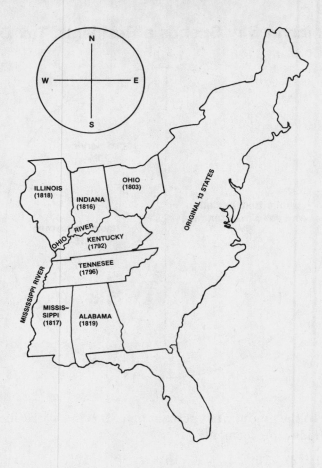

21. Which of the following would be the BEST title for the map?

    (1) States Added to the Original 13 States, 1800–1810
    (2) States Added to the Original 13 States, 1792–1819
    (3) The Original 13 States
    (4) States Along the Ohio River

22. According to the map, the Ohio River forms a southern border for which of the following three states?

    (1) Illinois, Indiana, Kentucky   (2) Illinois, Indiana, Tennessee
    (3) Illinois, Kentucky, Tennessee   (4) Illinois, Indiana, Ohio

23. According to the map, in what year did Ohio join the Union?

    (1) 1792   (2) 1796   (3) 1803   (4) 1816

24. From information on the map, you can conclude that after 1792 the country was generally growing

    (1) westward   (2) northward   (3) southward   (4) eastward

Check your answers on page 99.

PART C: SCIENCE

Use the illustrations to answer the questions.

FACTS ABOUT THE PLANETS

Planet	Diameter (in miles)	Number of Satellites	Sidereal Revolution	Average Distance from the Sun (in miles)
Mercury	3,100	0	88 days	36 million
Venus	?	0	225 days	67 million
Earth	8,000	1	365 days	93 million
Mars	4,200	2	687 days	141 million
Jupiter	88,000	16?	12 years	480 million
Saturn	71,000	16?	30 years	900 million
Uranus	32,000	5	84 years	1.8 billion
Neptune	31,000	3	164 years	2.8 billion
Pluto	1,500	1	248 years	5.9 billion

The sidereal revolution is the amount of time a planet takes to orbit the sun. The time is recorded in earth days or years.

1. According to the chart, which of the following planets has the largest diameter?

   (1) Neptune   (2) Uranus   (3) Saturn   (4) Jupiter

2. According to the chart, what is the sidereal revolution of Earth?

   (1) 365 days   (2) 687 days   (3) 12 years   (4) 30 years

3. According to the chart, how many satellites does Mars have?

   (1) 3   (2) 2   (3) 1   (4) none

4. According to information in the chart, which planet is closest to the sun?

   (1) Earth   (2) Jupiter   (3) Mercury   (4) Venus

MEASURING SOUND

Decibels	Description of Sound	Some Sources of Sounds
0–10	very faint	light breathing
10–25	faint	a whisper
25–50	moderate	quiet radio
50–70	loud	vacuum cleaner
70–90	very loud	power lawn mower
90–115	deafening	jackhammer
115–125	painful to hear	nearby thunder
125 or more	permanent hearing loss	bomb exploding

A decibel is a unit for measuring sound. The description of the sound applies when the sound is heard for a short time.

5. According to the chart, a sound at 30 decibels would be described as

   (1) very faint   (2) faint   (3) moderate   (4) loud

6. According to the chart, a jackhammer is an example of a noise described as

   (1) deafening   (2) very loud   (3) loud   (4) moderate

7. You can conclude that the sound of a feather dropping to the ground would probably have a decibel reading of about

   (1) 0–10   (2) 50–70   (3) 90–115   (4) 125 or more

8. According to the chart, which of the following sounds would create a permanent hearing loss after a short time?

   (1) a whisper   (2) a vacuum cleaner
   (3) a power mower   (4) a bomb exploding

Composition of the Atmosphere

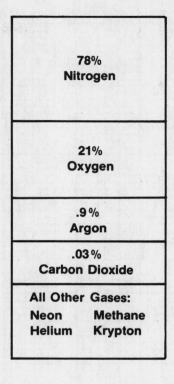

9. According to the graph, what percent of the atmosphere is nitrogen?

   (1) .1%   (2) .9%   (3) 21%   (4) 78%

10. According to the graph, which two gases make up most of the atmosphere?

    (1) nitrogen and argon   (2) argon and carbon dioxide
    (3) nitrogen and oxygen   (4) oxygen and argon

11. According to the graph, which of the following gases is found the least in the atmosphere?

    (1) nitrogen   (2) carbon dioxide   (3) argon   (4) oxygen

12. According to information in the graph, which of the following gases makes up .9% of the atmosphere?

    (1) carbon dioxide   (2) argon   (3) oxygen   (4) nitrogen

One Year's Monthly Rainfall in Seattle, Washington

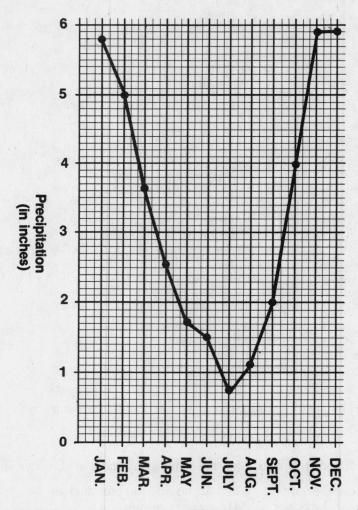

13. According to the graph, the number of inches of rainfall in Seattle in September was about

   (1) 5   (2) 4   (3) 3   (4) 2

14. According to the graph, there was more rain in the month of May than in the month of

   (1) March   (2) July   (3) October   (4) November

15. According to the graph, which of the following seasons had the most rain?

   (1) summer (June, July, August)
   (2) spring (March, April, May)
   (3) fall (September, October, November)
   (4) winter (December, January, February)

16. According to the graph, which month had a rainfall of about .7 inches?

   (1) February   (2) May   (3) July   (4) September

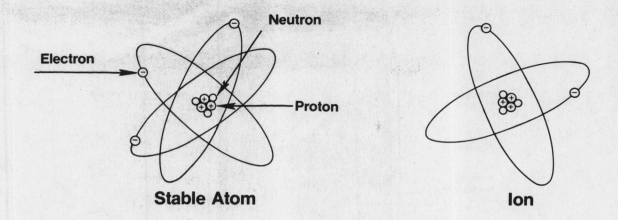

Stable Atom   **Ion**

An atom has three parts: protons, electrons, and neutrons. Protons have a positive charge. Electrons have a negative charge. When an atom has the same number of protons as electrons, it is stable. It has no electrical charge. When an atom gains or loses an electron, it becomes an ion. If an ion has more protons than electrons, it has a positive charge.

17. According to the diagrams, all of the following are parts of an atom EXCEPT

    (1) protons   (2) ions   (3) neutrons   (4) electrons

18. You can infer that the ion in the diagram has

    (1) a positive charge   (2) a negative charge
    (3) no charge   (4) a neutral charge

19. You can infer that the stable atom in the diagram

    (1) has a positive charge   (2) has a negative charge
    (3) is an ion   (4) has no electrical charge

20. You can conclude that if an atom has more electrons than protons then it

    (1) has a negative charge   (2) is stable
    (3) has a positive charge   (4) is not an ion

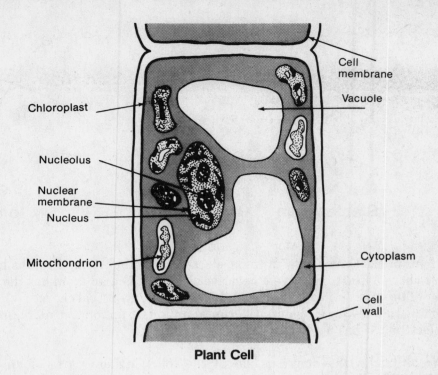

Plant Cell

The nucleus of a plant cell directs the cell's activities. The cytoplasm comprises everything within the cell wall that is not the nucleus. The cytoplasm is mostly water. Mitochondria release energy for the cell. Very active cells have many mitochondria. The cell membrane controls the flow of food and oxygen in and out of the cell. Chloroplasts are the areas where food is made. Vacuoles are usually filled with water or oils.

21. According to the diagram, the cell membrane is within the

    (1) vacuole   (2) cell wall
    (3) nucleolus   (4) mitochondria

22. According to the diagram, the nucleus surrounds the

    (1) cytoplasm   (2) vacuole
    (3) nucleolus   (4) cell wall

23. The cytoplasm includes all of the following EXCEPT

    (1) nucleus   (2) mitochondria
    (3) chloroplast   (4) vacuole

24. From the information, which of the following things do vacuoles and cytoplasm have in common?

    (1) They are both filled with oils.
    (2) They are both within the nucleus.
    (3) They may both contain water.
    (4) They both control the flow of food and oxygen.

Annual U.S. Deaths Due to Cardiovascular Diseases By Major Type of Disorder

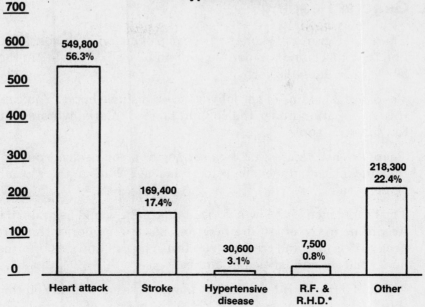

*Rheumatic Fever and Rheumatic Heart Disease.
Source: National Center for Health Statistics
U.S. Department of Health and Human Services

25. According to the graph, what percent of the people who die of cardiovascular disease die of hypertensive disease?

(1) .8% (2) 3.1% (3) 17.4% (4) 56.3%

26. According to the graph, how many people die of stroke in a year?

(1) 169,400 (2) 218,300 (3) 549,800 (4) 669,800

27. According to the graph, what is the most common disorder that leads to death by cardiovascular disease?

(1) rheumatic fever and rheumatic heart disease
(2) hypertensive disease
(3) stroke
(4) heart attack

28. According to the graph, which of the following disorders causes the least number of deaths?

(1) rheumatic fever and rheumatic heart disease
(2) hypertensive disease
(3) stroke
(4) heart attack

Check your answers on page 101.

ANSWERS AND EXPLANATIONS

Part A: General Reading

1. **(3)** There are 5 grams of protein in one cup of cream-style corn. You can find this information under the column labeled "Protein" in the row labeled "cream-style corn."

2. **(2)** There are 20 grams of carbohydrates in a single apple. You can find this information under the column labeled "Carbohydrates" in the row labeled "apple."

3. **(4)** There are no grams of fat in a serving of green beans. You can find this information under the column labeled "Fat" in the row labeled "green beans."

4. **(1)** The best choice for a low-calorie main course would be drained tuna. According to the chart, drained tuna has fewer calories than ground beef, coffeecake, and cream-style corn. You can find this information under the column labeled "Calories."

5. **(2)** About 400 people ride West City public buses at 6 AM. You can find this information by locating 6 AM at the bottom of the graph. Follow the 6 AM line up until it meets the line that shows usage. Then look at the number at the left. The number is 4, which stands for 400.

6. **(2)** About 200 people ride West City public buses at 8 PM. You can find this information by locating 8 PM at the bottom of the graph. Follow the 8 PM line up until it meets the line that shows usage. Then look at the number at the left. The number is 2, which stands for 200.

7. **(1)** You can infer that there are no public buses running in the city between 12 AM and 4 AM. The line that shows usage does not run between 12 AM and 4 AM. You can conclude that there are no riders at those hours because the buses are not running.

8. **(2)** You can conclude that the hours to add buses would be at 8 AM and 5 PM. According to the chart, the highest points of ridership are at 8 AM and 5 PM, when there are about 600 people riding the buses.

9. **(2)** It would cost a person living in Zone C $520 to heat his home with coal. You can find this information under the column labeled "C" in the row labeled "Coal."

10. **(1)** If a person living in Zone B changed from oil heat to gas heat, he could expect to save $185. Under Zone B, oil heat costs $700. Gas heat costs $515. The difference between $700 and $515 is $185.

11. **(3)** It would cost a person living in Zone D $760 to heat his home with gas. You can find this information under the column labeled "D" in the row labeled "Gas."

12. **(2)** You can infer that electricity is the most expensive fuel to use in all five zones. You can find this information by comparing the price of electricity to the four other types of fuel in each zone. Electricity is always the most expensive.

13. **(4)** The total number of feet needed to stop a car that is traveling at 50 miles per hour is 183 feet. You can find this information by reading the material that comes with the diagram. The last sentence says that the number at the top of each bar shows the total number of feet that it takes to stop the car. The number at the top of the bar labeled "50" is 183.

14. **(3)** The vehicle braking distance for a car that is traveling at 60 miles per hour is 185 feet. You can find this information in the diagram. The white area in the bar labeled "60" is the vehicle braking distance in feet. This white area shows 185 feet.

15. **(1)** The driver's thinking distance increases as the speed of the car increases. The driver's thinking distance at 20 miles per hour is 22 feet. The thinking distance increases up through 70 miles per hour, when the thinking distance is 77 feet.

16. **(2)** The speed of a vehicle has a direct effect on the distance needed to stop the vehicle. Both the driver's thinking distance and the vehicle braking distance increase as the speed of the car increases. You can find this information by comparing distances in the diagram.

17. **(4)** According to the fifth line in the chart, 1 liter equals 2.11 pints.

18. **(3)** According to the first line in the chart, 1 gallon equals 3.79 liters.

19. **(2)** You can infer that 2 quarts is equal to a little less than two liters. According to the second line in the chart, 1 quart equals .95 liters. 1 quart equals less than one liter. You can infer that 2 quarts equals less than 2 liters.

20. **(4)** You can conclude that the largest unit of measurement in the table is the kiloliter. According to the chart, 1 gallon equals 3.79 liters, but 1,000 liters equals 1 kiloliter.

Part B: Social Studies

1. **(4)** According to the table, the gross national product for Japan in 1980 was $990 billion. You can find this information under the column labeled "Gross National Product" in the row labeled "Japan."

2. **(3)** The table says that Norway had a per capita income of $7,949 in 1978. You can find this information under the column labeled "Per Capita Income" in the row labeled "Norway."

3. **(4)** The U.S.A. had the highest gross national product of all the nations in the table. According to the table, the U.S.A. had a gross national product of $2,576.6 billion in 1980. This is the highest gross national product figure in the table.

4. **(2)** You can conclude that the average person in Nigeria in 1978 earned less than $1,000. You can find this information under the column labeled "Per Capita Income" in the row labeled "Nigeria." According to the table, the per capita income in Nigeria in 1978 was $523. This means that the average person in Nigeria earned less than $1,000 that year.

5. **(1)** In 1830, there were more children under 5 years of age than in any other year in the graph. You can find this information under the column labeled "Under 5 Years" in the row labeled "1830."

6. **(3)** 24% of the U.S. population was between 45 and 64 years old in 1980. You can find this information under the column labeled "45–64" in the row labeled "1980." According to the graph, each figure represents about 6% of the U.S. population. Therefore, the four figures represent 24%.

7. **(3)** The largest age group in 1930 was the 20–44 group. You can find this information under the column labeled "20–44" in the row labeled "1930." According to the graph, 36% of the U.S. population in 1930 was aged 20–44. This is the largest age group the graph lists in 1930.

8. **(4)** You can conclude that the trend of the U.S. population on the whole is to have fewer children and to live longer. The number of children under 5 years of age has decreased from 1830 to 1980. The number of people 65 years of age and over has increased from 1830 to 1980.

9. **(3)** You can infer that over the last 10 years the number of all households in Mannix County has increased slightly. You can find this information by noting the slight incline in the line that stands for the total number of households.

10. **(1)** You can infer that over the last 10 years the number of households without children in Mannix County has increased greatly. You can find this information by noting the sharp incline in the line that stands for the number of households without children.

11. **(3)** You can infer that over the last 10 years the number of households with children in Mannix County has decreased greatly. You can find this information by noting the sharp decline in the line that stands for number of households with children.

12. **(1)** You can conclude that the number of households without children in Mannix County will increase. According to the graph, the number of households without children has increased greatly over the last 10 years. You can conclude that this trend will probably continue.

13. **(4)** There are 20,000 people of voting age in Gurney County. You can find this information at the top of the bar labeled "Number of People of Voting Age."

14. **(2)** 10,000 people were registered voters before the voting drive. You can find this information at the top of the bar labeled "Number of Registered Voters Before Drive."

15. **(3)** 15,000 people were registered voters after the voting drive. You can find this information at the top of the bar labeled Number of Registered Voters After Drive.

16. **(4)** You can conclude that the voting drive in Gurney County had increased the number of registered voters. You can find this information by comparing the number of registered voters before and after the drive. According to the graph, 5,000 more people were registered voters after the voting drive.

17. **(3)** 15% of a Marvin City resident's tax dollar is spent on law enforcement. You can find this information within the segment of the graph labeled "law enforcement."

18. **(1)** 20% of a Marvin City resident's tax dollar is spent on social services. You can find this information within the segment of the graph labeled "social services."

19. **(4)** The program that receives the least money from a Marvin City resident's tax dollar is recreation areas. You can find this information by comparing the percentages in the graph. The segment of the graph labeled "recreation areas" shows 5% of a resident's tax dollar. 5% is the smallest percentage in the graph.

20. **(1)** Public transportation and road maintenance use half of a Marvin City resident's tax dollar. You can find this information by comparing segments of the graph. Public transportation and road maintenance occupy half of the graph. Therefore, you can conclude that the programs use half of a resident's tax dollar.

21. **(2)** The best title for the map would be "States Added to the Original 13 States, 1792–1819." The map shows seven states that entered the Union from 1792 to 1819. The rest of the map is labeled "Original 13 States." Therefore, the best title would be "States Added to the Original 13 States, 1792–1819."

22. **(4)** The Ohio River forms a southern border for Illinois, Indiana, and Ohio. You can find this information in the map. The Ohio River flows south of these three states.

23. **(3)** Ohio joined the Union in 1803. You can find this information by reading the date printed below Ohio.

24. **(1)** You can conclude that after 1792 the country was generally growing westward. The compass next to the map indicates which direction is west. The new states are west of the original 13 states.

Part C: Science

1. **(4)** Jupiter has the largest diameter. You can find this information by comparing the diameters of the planets in the table. Jupiter has the largest diameter at 88,000 miles.

2. **(1)** The sidereal revolution of Earth is 365 days. You can find this information under the column labeled "Sidereal Revolution" in the row labeled "Earth."

3. **(2)** Mars has 2 satellites. You can find this information under the column labeled "Number of Satellites" in the row labeled "Mars."

4. **(3)** The closest planet to the sun is Mercury. According to the chart, Mercury has an average distance from the sun of 36 million miles. This is the shortest distance from the sun of all the planets.

5. **(3)** A sound at 30 decibels would be described as moderate. You can find this information under the column labeled "Description of Sound" in the row labeled "25–50" decibels.

6. **(1)** A jackhammer is an example of a noise described as deafening. You can find this information under the column labeled "Description of Sound" next to the word "jackhammer."

7. **(1)** You can conclude that the sound of a feather dropping to the ground would have a decibel reading of about 0–10. According to the graph, a sound at the decibel reading of 0–10 is described as very faint. A feather falling to the ground would make a very faint sound. Therefore, a feather dropping to the ground would have a decibel reading of about 0–10.

8. **(4)** A bomb exploding would create a permanent hearing loss after a short time. You can find this information under the column labeled "Description of Sound" next to the words "bomb exploding."

9. **(4)** According to the graph, 78% of the atmosphere is nitrogen.

10. **(3)** Nitrogen and oxygen make up most of the atmosphere. According to the graph, nitrogen makes up 78% of the atmosphere, and oxygen makes up 21% of the atmosphere. Together, nitrogen and oxygen make up 99% of the atmosphere.

11. **(2)** Of the four gases listed, carbon dioxide is found the least in the atmosphere. You can find this information by comparing the percentages of the gases in the atmosphere. According to the graph, carbon dioxide makes up .03% of the atmosphere. This is less than the amount of nitrogen, oxygen, or argon in the atmosphere.

12. **(2)** According to the graph, argon comprises .9% of the atmosphere.

13. **(4)** The number of inches of rainfall in September was 2 inches. You can find this information in the graph by noting where the line intersects the month and inches.

14. **(2)** There was more rain in the month of May than in the month of July. You can find this information in the graph by noting that about 2 inches of rain fell in May and less than 1 inch of rain fell in July.

15. **(4)** There was the most rain in the season of winter. You can find this information in the graph by noting that the line of the graph reaches its highest peaks in the winter months. There were about 6 inches of rain in December and January, and about 5 inches of rain in February.

16. **(3)** July had a rainfall of about .7 inches. You can find this information in the graph by noting where the line goes below 1 inch of rain. The only month that received less than 1 inch of rain is the month of July.

17. **(2)** Ions are NOT a part of an atom. According to the diagrams, atoms are made up of protons, neutrons, and electrons. Ions are not a part of an atom. They are atoms with electrical charges.

18. **(1)** You can infer that the ion in the diagram has a positive charge. The ion in the diagram has three protons and two electrons. Since the ion has more protons than electrons, it has a positive charge.

19. **(4)** You can infer that the stable atom in the diagram has no electrical charge. According to the information supplied with the diagram, when an atom has the same number of protons as electrons, it has no electrical charge.

20. **(1)** You can conclude that if an atom has more electrons than protons, then the atom has a negative charge. According to the information supplied with the diagram, when an ion has more protons than electrons, it has a positive charge. The information tells you that an electron has a negative charge. Therefore, you can conclude that an atom with more electrons than protons has a negative charge.

21. **(2)** The cell membrane is within the cell wall. You can find this information by examining the diagram.

22. **(3)** The nucleus surrounds the nucleolus. You can find this information by examining the diagram.

23. **(1)** The cytoplasm does not include the nucleus. You can find this by reading the information below the diagram. According to the information, the cytoplasm comprises everything within the cell wall except the nucleus.

24. **(3)** Vacuoles and cytoplasm may both contain water. You can find this by reading the information below the diagram. The information tells you that the cytoplasm is mostly water and vacuoles are usually filled with water or oils.

25. **(2)** 3.1% of the people who die of cardiovascular disease die of hypertensive disease. You can find this information by reading the percent above the bar labeled "Hypertensive Disease."

26. **(1)** 169,400 people die of stroke. You can find this information by reading the figure for the number of deaths above the bar labeled "Stroke."

27. **(4)** The most common disorder in the number of deaths by cardiovascular disease is heart attack. You can find this information by comparing the percents for each disorder. Heart attacks account for 56.3% of the deaths, more than any other disorder listed in the graph.

28. **(1)** Rheumatic fever and rheumatic heart disease occur less often than heart attack, stroke, or hypertensive disease. You can find this information by comparing the percents for each disorder. Only .8% of the people who die of cardiovascular disease die of rheumatic fever or rheumatic heart disease.

GENERAL REVIEW

PART A: GENERAL READING AND PROSE LITERATURE

Read each passage. Then choose the correct answer to each question that follows the passage.

MOVIE TIMETABLE

Colony Theater

Slow Pokes 1:40, 3:45, 5:50, 7:55

Mayberry Cinema

Rip Tide 1, 3, 5, 7, 9

Shirley Twin

Visitors from the Planet Zoltar 3:10, 5:15, 7:20, 9:40
Bear Hug 6, 8, 10, midnight

Movieland

Butler Place Beauties 2:20, 4:30, 6:40, 8:50

Cinema 59

I—Last Train to Parksville 2, 4, 6, 8
II—Jive Talk 2:45, 4:45, 6:45, 8:45
III—Bear Hug 1:30, 3:30, 5:30, 7:30
IV—Jive Talk 3, 5, 7, 9

1. According to the timetable, which movie is playing at the Mayberry Cinema?

   (1) Slow Pokes   (2) Visitors from the Planet Zoltar
   (3) Rip Tide   (4) Bear Hug

2. According to the timetable, what is the latest starting time for the movie *Bear Hug* at the Shirley Twin?

   (1) 9:40   (2) 10:00   (3) 10:30   (4) 12:00

3. According to the timetable, how many different films are being shown at Cinema 59?

   (1) one   (2) two   (3) three   (4) four

4. At 6:30, a man shows up at Cinema 59. According to the timetable, which is the first movie he can see from the start?

   (1) Last Train to Parksville   (2) Jive Talk
   (3) Bear Hug   (4) Butler Place Beauties

Mrs. T's Chuck Wagon Chili

1 clove garlic, chopped
1 onion, chopped
1 green bell pepper, chopped
2 tablespoons cooking oil
1 pound ground beef
$1\frac{1}{2}$ tablespoons chili powder
1 teaspoon crushed red pepper
8 ounces tomato sauce
1 can kidney beans (15 ounces)
$\frac{1}{2}$ bottle beer (6 ounces)

1. Heat the cooking oil in a large pot. Add the garlic, onion, and green bell pepper. Cook until onion is wilted and pepper is soft.

2. Add the ground beef to the garlic, onion, and pepper. Cook the ground beef until it is browned.

3. After the ground beef has been browned, drain the oil from the pot. Then return the pot to the stove.

4. Stir the chili powder and crushed red pepper into the ground beef, garlic, onion, and pepper mixture.

5. Add the tomato sauce, kidney beans, and beer to the mixture. Cook over low heat until the beer evaporates.

Serve with shredded cheese or sour cream topping. Makes 2 servings.

5. How much chili powder is needed to make two servings of Mrs. T's Chuck Wagon Chili?

    (1) 1 teaspoon   (2) $1\frac{1}{2}$ tablespoons
    (3) 2 tablespoons   (4) 3 tablespoons

6. According to the recipe, when is the ground beef added?

    (1) before the onion is wilted
    (2) before the cooking oil is heated
    (3) after the green bell pepper gets soft
    (4) after the tomato sauce is added

7. From the recipe, you can infer that Mrs. T's Chuck Wagon Chili should be served

    (1) right after the ground beef has been browned
    (2) after the tomato sauce has evaporated
    (3) after the beer has evaporated
    (4) before the chili powder is stirred into the mixture

8. If Mrs. T wanted to make four servings of chili, how much ground beef would she need?

    (1) one pound   (2) two pounds
    (3) four pounds   (4) six pounds

When Maude Lessing opened her newspaper to read the Dear Babs column, she got a bit of a shock. Her letter to Dear Babs, the marriage advice columnist, was printed in the paper. But Maude had written her letter fifteen years ago.

"She printed an old letter and old advice," Maude told reporters last week. "And it's wrecked my marriage."

Fifteen years ago, Maude Lessing wrote to Dear Babs about her troubled marriage to Orville Lessing. In the letter, Maude called her husband a gambler and a drunk. Dear Babs quickly published the letter, with the advice that Maude leave her husband. Maude had shown Orville the letter and the advice. "He was a perfect husband after that," says Maude.

But now, fifteen years later, Dear Babs reprinted the letter and the advice.

"I guess Orville read it again, because he's gone," says Maude. "He must have thought I'd written to Babs to tell her he hadn't changed after fifteen years. I'd like to bring that Babs into court."

Dear Babs, whose real name is Elaine Hipswitch, had this comment: "Mrs. Lessing had never signed her letter. I wouldn't have known whom to write to for permission to reprint it. Besides, the moment I receive a letter it becomes my personal property. I own every letter to Babs."

Other readers of Dear Babs have started to question Ms. Hipswitch's habit of "recycling" letters. "I don't like you publishing old problems," one reader wrote to Babs. "I want to read about modern problems."

"There's no such thing as a new marriage problem," Babs wrote in reply.

Maude Lessing urges readers not to read the Dear Babs column until Ms. Hipswitch agrees to print only recent letters.

9. According to the passage, Maude Lessing wants readers to stop reading Dear Babs because Elaine Hipswitch

    (1) called Lessing's husband a gambler and a drunk
    (2) gives bad advice
    (3) reprints old letters
    (4) doesn't ask for permission when she prints a letter

10. Based on the information in the passage, with which of the following statements would Elaine Hipswitch most likely agree?

    (1) There are new kinds of marital problems in society.
    (2) A wife should leave her husband if he is a gambler and a drunk.
    (3) People shouldn't interfere in other people's problems.
    (4) Orville Lessing never changed in 15 years.

11. Which of the following statements from the passage is an opinion?

    (1) Dear Babs reprints old letters for her column.
    (2) Orville Lessing read the reprint of his wife's letter.
    (3) All letters to Dear Babs become Hipswitch's property.
    (4) Dear Babs advised Maude Lessing to leave her husband.

12. Which of the following words best describes Maude Lessing's feelings toward Dear Babs?

    (1) disappointment   (2) admiration
    (3) gratefulness   (4) anger

Year after year, Anson City residents ask the same question. Should the city legalize gambling?

"Why not?" says city councilmember Vernon Hess. "People gamble anyway. Why shouldn't the city benefit?"

"This was a major campaign issue," says Mayor John Woolcot. "I have not changed my position. Anson City will maintain its standards."

Hess and other councilmembers propose a "Venture Center." The center would have a race track and a casino. Hess likes to call the casino the "Winning Palace." The "Winning Palace" would have blackjack tables and slot machines.

Hess would also like a lottery. "The state has a lottery. Why shouldn't the city have one? The state makes $80 million a year. The city could make $15 million a year." (The mayor's office puts the estimated figure at $9 million.)

Woolcot claims that legalized gambling leads to illegal activities. Organized crime moves in. "The city would still need high taxes. The taxes would go towards law enforcement. Police would be needed to fight against organized crime." Woolcot adds that there is no proof legalized gambling reduces illegal gambling.

Where would Venture Center go? Hess likes the South Grove section of the city. But many South Grove residents oppose the center. They say there is not enough public transportation. There are not enough parking spaces. They say there is no room for the center.

But there are other people who want the center very much. The Mahan hotel chain is interested. The Anson Senior League is interested, too. "Seniors need relaxation," said a spokeswoman. "Venture Center sounds like a good bet."

13. Which of the following is NOT stated as a reason that South Grove residents oppose Venture Center?

   (1) Organized crime would move into South Grove.
   (2) There isn't enough additional parking.
   (3) There isn't enough room for the center in the community.
   (4) There isn't enough public transportation.

14. Based on the passage, with which of the following statements about legalized gambling would Vernon Hess most likely agree?

   (1) Legalized gambling reduces illegal gambling.
   (2) Legalized gambling attracts organized crime.
   (3) Legalized gambling would destroy family life in Anson City.
   (4) Legalized gambling would require an increase in the police force.

15. Which of the following statements from the passage is a fact?

   (1) The Mahan hotel chain is interested in Venture Center.
   (2) Anson City could make $15 million a year from a lottery.
   (3) Anson City would benefit from legalized gambling.
   (4) Senior citizens would enjoy Venture Center.

16. Which of the following is the BEST title for the passage?

   (1) Opposition to Gambling
   (2) Anson City and Organized Crime
   (3) The Anson City Gambling Debate
   (4) The "Winning Palace"

"What did you say your name was?" the sheriff asked.

"Arnold," he replied; but he could not remember telling the sheriff his name before.

"Curwing?"

"Yes."

"What were you doing with a .22, Arnold?"

"It's mine," he said.

"Okay. What were you going to shoot?"

"Some ducks," he replied.

"Out of season?"

He nodded.

"That's bad," said the sheriff. "Were you and your brother good friends?"

What did he mean — good friends? Eugie was his brother. That was different from a friend, Arnold thought. A best friend was your own age, but Eugie was almost a man. Eugie had had a way of looking at him, slyly and mockingly and yet confidentially, that had summed up how they both felt about being brothers. Arnold had wanted to be with Eugie more than with anybody else but he couldn't say they had been good friends.

"Did they ever quarrel?" the sheriff asked his father.

"Not that I know," his father replied. "It seemed to me that Arnold cared a lot for Eugie."

"Did you?" the sheriff asked Arnold.

If it seemed so to his father, then it was so. Arnold nodded.

"Were you mad at him this morning?"

"No."

"How did you happen to shoot him?"

"We was crawlin' through the fence."

"Yes?"

"An' the gun got caught on the wire."

17. From the information in the passage, you can infer that a ".22" is

    (1) a fence   (2) a gun   (3) a wire   (4) a duck

18. You can conclude that the sheriff was asking Arnold the questions because

    (1)   Arnold was hunting ducks out of season
    (2)   Arnold shot his brother Eugie
    (3)   the sheriff did not know Arnold
    (4)   Arnold and his brother were caught trespassing

19. Which of the following statements about Arnold's feelings toward Eugie is supported by the passage?

    (1)   Arnold was mad at Eugie earlier in the morning.
    (2)   Arnold liked being Eugie's brother.
    (3)   Arnold felt that Eugie was his best friend.
    (4)   Arnold felt that Eugie was trying to get him in trouble.

There were a number of people out this afternoon, far more than last Sunday. And the band sounded louder and gayer. That was because the Season had begun. For although the band played all the year round on Sundays, out of season it was never the same. It was like some one playing with only the family to listen; it didn't care how it played if there weren't any strangers present. Wasn't the conductor wearing a new coat, too? She was sure it was new. He scraped with his foot and flapped his arms like a rooster about to crow, and the bandsmen sitting in the green rotunda blew out their cheeks and glared at the music. Now there came a little "flutey" bit — very pretty! — a little chain of bright drops. She was sure it would be repeated. It was; she lifted her head and smiled.

Only two people shared her "special" seat: a fine old man in a velvet coat, his hands clasped over a huge carved walking-stick, and a big old woman, sitting upright, with a roll of knitting on her embroidered apron. They did not speak. This was disappointing, for Miss Brill always looked forward to the conversation. She had become really quite expert, she thought, at listening as though she didn't listen, at sitting in other people's lives just for a minute while they talked round her.

20. From the information in the passage, you can infer that Miss Brill is

    (1) attending a concert   (2) riding on a train
    (3) visiting a relative   (4) going to church

21. The passage states that Miss Brill was disappointed because

    (1) the band did not play any music
    (2) she did not know anyone
    (3) the man and the woman were not speaking
    (4) the weather was rainy

22. Which of the following statements about Miss Brill is NOT supported by the passage?

    (1) Miss Brill likes to listen to the band play.
    (2) Miss Brill thinks that the band plays better during the Season.
    (3) Miss Brill likes to sit by herself during the band concert.
    (4) Miss Brill thought that the conductor was wearing a new coat.

Check your answers on page 118.

PART B: SOCIAL STUDIES

Read each passage. Then choose the correct answer to each question that follows the passage.

In the 1800's, trains blared and roared into stations. They were symbols of progress and expansion. They played as much of a role in America's history as presidents and generals.

The first American railroads were built in the late 1820's. The early railroads provided cheap transportation for shippers and travelers. To encourage the railroads to expand into unsettled lands, President Millard Fillmore signed a series of land-grant acts in the 1850's. These acts gave the railroads ownership of land that ran along the railways. In return for the land, the railroads carried government traffic at reduced rates. The railroads sold much of their land to farmers and cattlemen, who then shipped their goods on the trains.

The importance of the railroads became clear during the Civil War. During the war, trains carried troops, arms, and supplies. One reason that the North won the war is that it had more use of the railroads.

Between 1865 and 1900, railroads grew rapidly. The first transcontinental route was completed in 1869. This track made it easier for pioneers to cross the Rocky Mountains and settle the West. And the railroads brought new people to the West even before the trains started running. Thousands of Chinese and Irish immigrants helped to lay down the tracks.

1. Which of the following BEST expresses the main idea of the passage?

   (1) Trains brought progress and expansion to the U.S.
   (2) Railroads helped pioneers to cross the Rocky Mountains.
   (3) Railroads transported livestock and grain.
   (4) Railroads grew rapidly between 1865 and 1900.

2. According to the passage, which of the following statements does NOT describe a result of the land-grant acts of the 1850's?

   (1) The railroads expanded into unsettled territory.
   (2) Farmers and settlers received free land.
   (3) The government received reduced rates from the railroad.
   (4) The railroad made money from settlers who shipped goods on trains.

3. It can be inferred that the author believes that the railroads

   (1) ruined the West
   (2) provide the most important form of transportation today
   (3) cheated the government
   (4) improved life in America

4. Which of the following statements about railroads CANNOT be concluded from the passage?

   (1) Railroads carried Northern supplies during the Civil War.
   (2) Railroads provided farmers and cattlemen with an easier way to get goods to the market.
   (3) Railroads charged the government to ship government supplies.
   (4) Railroads did not bring new settlers to the West.

Until 1920, half of the adult population of the United States could not vote. Women's fight for suffrage, or the right to vote, was won slowly.

The first Woman's Rights Convention was held in Seneca Falls, New York, in 1848. Elizabeth Cady Stanton was the organizer. Stanton believed that all adult citizens, regardless of their sex, had the right to vote. She protested unfair laws. In Stanton's time, married women were not allowed to own property. They couldn't own the money that they earned. And if a woman was divorced or deserted by her husband, she couldn't have custody of her children. Stanton believed that women could change these laws if they could vote.

Many men opposed suffrage. Some men thought women would vote too radically. Liquor manufacturers thought that women would vote for prohibition. Some manufacturers thought that suffragists would try to raise the wages of women factory workers. Many women opposed suffrage, also. Some of them were afraid that they would be expected to work outside the home.

Elizabeth Cady Stanton worked with a younger woman, Susan B. Anthony. Stanton and Anthony read about the tactics of suffragists in England. English suffragists had gone on hunger strikes and battled with police. They received publicity, but it was not all favorable. Anthony and Stanton took a different route. They spoke before legislative bodies. They held large, quiet marches through Washington and other cities.

Neither woman lived to see the dream of suffrage fulfilled. It was not until August 18, 1920, that the Nineteenth Amendment to the Constitution was passed, guaranteeing women the right to vote.

5. The passage states that in Stanton's time married women did not have the right to

    (1) raise their children   (2) work outside the home
    (3) own property   (4) be divorced

6. The passage implies that Anthony and Stanton held quiet marches because

    (1) legislative bodies would not listen to them
    (2) marches disrupt the work of manufacturers
    (3) they did not want to starve on a hunger strike
    (4) violent tactics of English suffragists had not gotten favorable publicity

7. With which of the following statements would Elizabeth Cady Stanton have most likely agreed?

    (1) All men opposed suffrage.
    (2) All adult citizens should have the right to vote.
    (3) All women should work outside the home.
    (4) Women's fight for suffrage was won quickly.

8. Which of the following would be the BEST title for the passage?

    (1) Stanton and the Fight for Suffrage
    (2) Laws Unfair to Women
    (3) Women Before 1920
    (4) Women's Rights

The economic theories of John Maynard Keynes (1883–1946) have influenced governments in many nations, including the United States. Keynes believed in the capitalist system, but he suggested ways that the system could be improved. He was most concerned with how to boost national income and lower national unemployment.

The capitalist system is based on the idea that individuals, and not government, should control business and industry. Before Keynes, most capitalist economists believed that government should not get involved in the economy. In the beginning of his career, Keynes also believed that a free economy could solve most economic problems. However, as unemployment grew in England, Keynes began to think that government should play a part in shaping the economy.

Keynes thought that government could improve economic conditions by funding public works projects. Public works projects would improve the economy by employing people to build bridges, dams, roads, and housing projects. Private industry would benefit from the projects because the government would buy materials from businesses. These businesses would need to employ more workers to produce the additional goods.

Keynes also thought that the government should regulate trade. He thought that a government should protect business in its own country by taxing and limiting imports.

9. According to the passage, the main difference between Keynes's ideas and the ideas of traditional capitalists is that Keynes wanted government to

(1) take over business and industry
(2) stay out of the economy
(3) get involved in the economy
(4) strengthen trade with other nations

10. It can be inferred from the passage that a "free economy" is an economy that

(1) is not subject to government involvement
(2) has high unemployment
(3) depends on public works projects
(4) does not use money

11. All of the following are stated in the passage as benefits of public works projects EXCEPT

(1) increased work for private industry
(2) new roads, dams, and housing for the people
(3) lowered inflation
(4) lowered unemployment

12. It can be inferred from the passage that Keynes thought government should tax and limit imports because imports

(1) hurt business in the country receiving the imports
(2) raised consumer prices
(3) interfered with a free economy
(4) interfered with public works projects

Everyone knows that Miami Beach, Florida, is different from Juneau, Alaska. But exactly how and why are they different? What is it about the two places that makes them so different? Geographers study the characteristics of places to find answers to these questions. They study the physical, biotic, and cultural patterns of the earth's surface.

Physical patterns include the distribution of landforms, soils, water, features, and climates. Biotic patterns include the distribution of animals and plants. Cultural patterns include the distribution of such man-made features as cities, farms, and roads. Geographers make maps of all of these patterns. The maps are useful not only to geographers but also to other scientists, governments, business, and travelers.

There are many different specialities within the field of geography. Industrial geographers, for example, help businesses decide where to build their manufacturing plants. They consider the location of raw materials, the work force, and roadways when they do their planning. Historical geographers study how places have changed over time. They study written records and the land itself to put together descriptions of how a place was in the past. Climatologists study the world's climates. They map, compare, and analyze the distribution of various climates. Climatologists and meteorologists, scientists who study weather patterns, help each other with their work.

Industrial geography, historical geography, and climatology are just a few of the many branches of geography. But each branch of geography is united in an attempt to help us see patterns in the geosphere, or earth.

13. It can be inferred from the passage that climatologists are most interested in the earth's

    (1) biotic patterns
    (2) cultural patterns
    (3) physical patterns
    (4) industrial patterns

14. Which of the following is an example of a biotic difference between Alaska and Florida?

    (1) There are seals and bears in Alaska, but they don't inhabit Florida.
    (2) The climate is cold in Alaska but warm in Florida.
    (3) There are fewer cities in Alaska than there are in Florida.
    (4) There are mountain ranges in Alaska, but there aren't any mountains in Florida.

15. The main idea of the passage is that geographers

    (1) look for patterns in the earth's surface
    (2) make maps
    (3) help businesses decide where to build factories
    (4) study how places have changed over time

16. The word "geosphere" most nearly means

    (1) "earth"   (2) "animals and plants"
    (3) "man-made features"   (4) "climate"

Amy Rand is a sociology student at Handel State College. Rand has a theory. She thinks that a person who commits a crime while he is part of a mob is not guilty of the crime. Amy thinks that when "John Doe" is alone, he is John Doe. But when he is in a mob, John Doe becomes someone else. That "someone else" is guilty of the crime, not John Doe.

Sociologists separate crowds into two groups. There are expressive crowds and active crowds. In an expressive crowd, people sit or stand close to one another. They act openly. They may be loud and energetic. They react on the spur of the moment. An example of an expressive crowd is a group of fans at a football game. Amy Rand feels that John Doe is different in an expressive crowd. He is noisier than usual. But he is still himself.

An active crowd is an expressive crowd taken a step further. An active crowd takes action. When the Pope came to America, he was met by expressive crowds. The people cheered. Then they surged through police lines. They knocked over barriers. They became an active crowd. Amy thinks John Doe would be more active than usual in an active crowd. But he would not become someone else until he was in a mob.

When there is tension, an active crowd can become a mob. A mob often commits violent acts. A mob may throw bricks at police or even kill an innocent man. People take on the anger of those around them. They do not think for themselves. Amy Rand thinks that this is when people stop being themselves. She thinks people shouldn't be held responsible for their actions when this happens.

17. According to the passage, an active crowd becomes a mob when

   (1) there is tension   (2) police are nearby
   (3) there is too much noise (4) crimes are committed

18. Which of the following statements from the passage is a fact?

   (1) When he is in a mob, John Doe becomes someone else.
   (2) People stop being themselves in mobs.
   (3) When "John Doe" is alone, he is John Doe.
   (4) Sociologists separate crowds into two groups.

19. Given the information in the passage, which of the following is an example of an expressive crowd?

   (1) fans breaking through police lines
   (2) patients sitting in a doctor's waiting room
   (3) spectators watching a horse race
   (4) a mob rioting in the street

20. With which of the following statements would Amy Rand most likely agree?

   (1) "John Doe" always becomes somebody else when he is in a crowd.
   (2) People should not always be held responsible for their actions when they are in mobs.
   (3) People are usually quiet and peaceful in expressive crowds.
   (4) A person who commits a crime is never guilty of the crime.

Check your answers on page 120.

PART C: SCIENCE

Read each passage. Then choose the correct answer to each question that follows the passage.

According to many scientists, the earth is about $4\frac{1}{2}$ billion years old. The first forms of life appeared on earth about 3 billion years ago. Since that time, there have been many different kinds of plants and animals on earth. Most of them no longer exist.

When a species of plant or animal dies out, it is said to be extinct. What causes a species to become extinct? The major reason is that the environment of the species changed. It changed to the extent that the species could no longer survive. For example, many kinds of dinosaurs once roamed the land that is now North America. When the dinosaurs lived, the environment suited their needs. But the environment changed. Changes in the earth's crust caused swamps to drain. This destroyed the natural habitat of many dinosaurs. The rise of mountains in North America also killed off many dinosaurs. The mountains caused the climate to become colder. In other parts of North America, floods killed many dinosaurs. Over time, dinosaurs also ran out of food. Many dinosaurs were plant-eating animals. Plants that they ate were being eaten up by smaller, quicker animals. The dinosaurs that could not compete with smaller animals for food died out.

Changes in the environment can cause the extinction of a species. But other factors can also cause a species to die out. The dodo was a species of bird that lived on some islands off the coast of Africa. The islands became a stopping point for sailors from Europe after 1500. Before the first sailors landed on the islands, the dodo was a common bird. But the sailors found that the dodo was a good source of food. Within 200 years, the dodo became extinct. The species was unable to survive the sailors' hunting.

1. According to the passage, the major reason that a species becomes extinct is

    (1) a change in its environment   (2) the rise of mountains
    (3) changes in the earth's crust   (4) hunting by humans

2. The word "extinct" most nearly means

    (1) "kill"   (2) "roam"   (3) "die out"   (4) "change"

3. From the information in the passage, you can infer that many dinosaurs lived

    (1) on mountains   (2) in swamps
    (3) on islands   (4) in cold areas

4. In the passage, the dodo is used to show how a species can become extinct because of

    (1) climate   (2) changes in the natural environment
    (3) floods   (4) humans

Diabetes is a serious health problem in the United States. More than 30,000 people die from the disease every year. About 4% of all women and 2% of all men will get diabetes in their lifetime.

One form of diabetes occurs when the body does not produce enough insulin. Insulin is a hormone. It is produced by the body's pancreas. The pancreas secretes insulin into the bloodstream. The insulin is important for controlling the level of glucose in the blood. Glucose is a sugar. It is the body's main source of food. If the body does not produce enough insulin, the level of glucose in the blood becomes high. A chronic shortage of the hormone insulin results in diabetes.

Diabetes is a serious disease, but it is not untreatable. If they get proper medication, diabetics can lead normal lives. A person who suffers from a severe case of diabetes can be injected with insulin every day. The injections of insulin keep the diabetic alive. Some diabetics can be treated with oral medication.

If diabetes is not treated, serious health problems can arise. Hyperglycemia is the condition of having too high a level of glucose in the blood. If the condition of hyperglycemia is not treated, heart disease can result. Uncontrolled diabetes also leads to a condition known as diabetic acidosis. Diabetic acidosis leads to death.

5. The main purpose of the passage is to describe

(1) diabetes   (2) insulin   (3) hormones   (4) hyperglycemia

6. According to the passage, glucose is

(1) a hormone   (2) a disease   (3) a medication   (4) a sugar

7. Which of the following statements about diabetes is NOT supported by the information in the passage?

(1) Diabetes is a serious disease.
(2) If it is not controlled, diabetes can lead to death.
(3) There are no treatments for diabetes.
(4) Diabetes can lead to heart disease.

8. A person who suffers from diabetes might be injected with insulin because

(1) his body is not producing enough insulin on its own
(2) there is a shortage of glucose in his blood
(3) there is a shortage of food in his blood
(4) the insulin helps the pancreas to produce glucose

Atoms are made up of three basic parts: protons, neutrons, and electrons. Protons and neutrons make up an atom's nucleus, or center. Protons have a positive electrical charge. Neutrons have no charge. Electrons are particles that circle around the atom's nucleus. Electrons have a negative electrical charge.

All atoms are made up of these basic particles. (The only exception to this is a hydrogen atom. An atom of common hydrogen does not contain any neutrons.) This means that everything is made up of protons, neutrons, and electrons. Oxygen is an element. It is made up of protons, neutrons, and electrons. Aluminum is an element. It also is made up of protons, neutrons, and electrons. What makes oxygen different from aluminum? What makes one element different from another one?

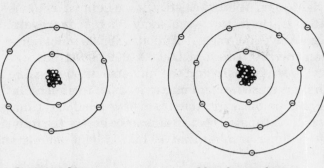

Oxygen Atom   **Aluminum Atom**

The answer is very simple. The main difference between atoms of one element and atoms of another element is the number of particles that the atoms contain. An atom of oxygen contains 8 protons, 8 neutrons, and 8 electrons. This combination of particles gives oxygen its qualities. On the other hand, one atom of aluminum contains 13 protons, 13 neutrons, and 13 electrons. This combination gives aluminum its qualities.

9. The main idea of the passage is that elements are different from one another because they have different

   (1) kinds of protons, neutrons, and electrons
   (2) numbers of protons, neutrons, and electrons
   (3) arrangements of protons, neutrons, and electrons
   (4) sizes of protons, neutrons, and electrons

10. Which of the following statements about elements is supported by the information in the passage?

   (1) All solid elements contain exactly 13 protons.
   (2) The atoms of most elements contain more protons than electrons.
   (3) Different elements contain different sizes of protons, neutrons, and electrons.
   (4) All elements are made up of the same basic particles.

11. From the diagram, you can infer that the symbol ⊖ stands for

   (1) a proton   (2) a neutron   (3) an electron   (4) an atom

12. The passage states that the nucleus of an atom contains

   (1) protons only
   (2) neutrons only
   (3) protons and neutrons only
   (4) protons, neutrons, and electrons

How do you measure distance? The most basic way to measure a distance is by measuring the amount of space between two points. For example, the distance from the top of this page to the bottom of this page is a little less than 11 inches. The distance between New York City and Los Angeles is about 2,500 miles. The distance between the earth and the moon is about 240,000 miles.

Measuring space is one way to measure a distance. But scientists have another way to measure distance. They measure distance with time. They measure distance with "light years."

What is a light year? Why do scientists use light years to measure distance? A light year stands for the distance that a ray of light can travel in a regular earth year. A ray of light travels at a speed of about 186,000 miles per second. In a year, a ray of light can travel 6 trillion (6,000,000,000,000) miles.

Scientists who study space and the universe often measure long distances. Using light years as a measurement makes it easier to understand and work with the distances. For example, some scientists have tried to estimate the size of the universe. They have estimated that the distance across the universe is 10 billion light years. The number of miles that 10 billion light years stands for is a "1" followed by 25 zeroes.

To understand the distance that is represented by a light year, think about this. The distance between the earth and the sun is about 93 million miles. This great distance only represents $8\frac{1}{3}$ minutes when it is measured in light years.

13. The main purpose of the passage is to explain

    (1) mileage   (2) space   (3) the universe   (4) light years

14. According to the passage, how many miles can a ray of light travel in one year?

    (1) 186,000   (2) 240,000   (3) 10 billion   (4) 6 trillion

15. Based on the information in the passage, how long would it take a ray of light to travel from the earth to the moon?

    (1) less than 2 seconds   (2) about 30 seconds
    (3) about 1 minute   (4) about 4 minutes

16. Which of the following statements about light years is supported by the passage?

    (1) The only way to measure distance in space is to use light years.
    (2) Using light years makes it easier to measure great distances.
    (3) A light year is not a reliable way to measure distances in space.
    (4) Light years are taking the place of inches and miles as a form of measurement.

Check your answers on page 122.

ANSWERS AND EXPLANATIONS

Part A: General Reading and Prose Literature

1. **(3)** *Rip Tide* is playing at the Mayberry Cinema. You can find this information in the fourth line of the timetable, under "Mayberry Cinema."

2. **(4)** The latest starting time for the movie *Bear Hug* at the Shirley Twin is midnight, or 12:00. You can find this information in line 7 under "Shirley Twin."

3. **(3)** Three different films are being shown at Cinema 59: *Last Train to Parksville, Jive Talk,* and *Bear Hug.* You can find this information in lines 11–14 of the timetable, under "Cinema 59."

4. **(2)** The first movie that the man can see from the start at Cinema 59 is *Jive Talk.* There is a 6:45 showing of *Jive Talk.* The other movies have showings at 7:00, 7:30, and 8:00. You can find this information in lines 11–14 under "Cinema 59."

5. **(2)** One-and-a-half tablespoons of chili powder is needed to make two servings of Mrs. T's Chuck Wagon Chili. You can find this information in the sixth line of the ingredients list.

6. **(3)** According to the recipe, ground beef is added after the green bell pepper gets soft. Step 1 tells you to cook the mixture until the pepper is soft. Step 2 tells you to add the ground beef to the mixture.

7. **(3)** You can infer from the recipe that the chili should be served after the beer has evaporated. The last step tells you to cook the chili until the beer evaporates. You can infer that the chili is ready to be served after the beer evaporates.

8. **(2)** If Mrs. T wanted to make four servings of chili, she would need two pounds of ground beef. The last line tells you that the ingredients in the recipe are for two servings. Line 5 of the ingredients list tells you that you need one pound of beef for two servings. To double the servings, you would double the ingredients.

9. **(3)** According to the passage, Maude Lessing wants readers to stop reading Dear Babs because Elaine Hipswitch reprints old letters. The last paragraph tells you that Maude Lessing urges readers not to read Dear Babs until Hipswitch argrees to print only recent letters.

10. **(2)** Based on the information in the passage, Elaine Hipswitch would most likely agree with the statement that a wife should leave her husband if he is a gambler and a drunk. The second paragraph tells you that Maude Lessing wrote Dear Babs and said that her husband was a gambler and a drunk. Dear Babs advised Lessing to leave her husband.

11. **(2)** The statement that Orville Lessing read the reprint of his wife's letter is an opinion. In the fifth paragraph, Maude Lessing says that she thinks her husband read the reprint. This is an opinion because there is no proof that her husband read the letter.

12. **(4)** The word "anger" best describes Maude Lessing's feelings toward Dear Babs. In the fifth paragraph, Lessing says that she'd "like to bring that Babs into court." You can tell from this statement that Lessing is angry at Babs.

13. **(1)** Fear of organized crime is NOT stated as a reason that South Grove residents oppose Venture Center. The reasons that South Grove residents oppose Venture Center are given in paragraph 8.

14. **(1)** Based on the information in the passage, Vernon Hess would most likely agree with the statement that legalized gambling reduces illegal gambling. The second paragraph tells you that Hess is in favor of legalized gambling. He implies in the second paragraph that people who gamble illegally would gamble legally, and the city would make money from them. You can infer that Hess thinks legalized gambling would reduce illegal gambling.

15. **(1)** The statement that the Mahan hotel chain is interested in Venture Center is a fact. Paragraph 9 tells you that the chain is interested in Venture Center.

16. **(3)** The best title for the passage is "The Anson City Gambling Debate." The passage describes the arguments for and against legalized gambling in Anson City.

17. **(2)** From the information in the passage, you can infer that a ".22" is a gun. In the seventh paragraph, the sheriff asks Arnold what he was going to shoot with the .22. You can infer from this information that a .22 is a gun.

18. **(2)** You can conclude that the sheriff was asking Arnold the questions because Arnold shot his brother Eugie. In the fourth-to-last paragraph, the sheriff asks Arnold, "How did you happen to shoot him?" Most of the questions the sheriff asks are about Arnold and his brother, so you can infer that the sheriff was investigating something that happened between the two of them.

19. **(2)** The passage supports the statement that Arnold liked being Eugie's brother. In paragraph 12, the author tells you that Arnold had wanted to be with Eugie more than anybody else.

20. **(1)** From the information in the passage, you can infer that Miss Brill is attending a concert. The first paragraph describes Miss Brill's thoughts about the band and the music. The second paragraph describes her seat at the concert.

21. **(3)** The passage states that Miss Brill was disappointed because the man and the woman were not speaking. The second paragraph tells you that Miss Brill shared her seat with two people. She was disappointed that they were not speaking because she liked listening to other people's conversations.

22. **(3)** The passage does NOT support the statement that Miss Brill likes to sit by herself during the band concert. The second paragraph tells you that Miss Brill enjoys listening to the people that sit with her during the band concert.

Part B: Social Studies

1. **(1)** The main idea of the passage is that trains brought progress and expansion to the U.S. The first paragraph tells you that trains were symbols of progress and expansion. The rest of the passage explains how the railroads grew and how they helped America to grow.

2. **(2)** The passage does not say that farmers and settlers received free land. The last sentence of paragraph 2 tells you that the railroads sold much of their land to farmers and cattlemen.

3. **(4)** You can infer that the author believes that the railroads helped to improve life in America. The author tells about many of the improvements that railroads made, such as providing cheap transportation and making it easier for settlers to move West.

4. **(4)** The statement that railroads did not bring new settlers to the West cannot be concluded from the passage. The passage states that the transcontinental railroad made it easier for people to move West. From this, you can conclude that the railroad *did* bring new settlers West.

5. **(3)** The passage states that married women did not have the right to own property in Stanton's time. You can find this information in paragraph 2.

6. **(4)** The passage implies that Anthony and Stanton held quiet marches because the tactics of the English suffragists had gotten bad publicity. In paragraph 4, it is stated that the English suffragists had battled with police. It also states that not all the publicity they received was favorable. It states that Anthony and Stanton decided not to do things the way that the English suffragists did. You can infer from this that they wanted to avoid getting bad publicity.

7. **(2)** Elizabeth Cady Stanton would have agreed with the statement that all adult citizens have the right to vote. Paragraph 2 states that Stanton believed this.

8. **(1)** Of the four titles, the best would be "Stanton and the Fight for Suffrage." The passage is mainly about Elizabeth Cady Stanton and her fight for women's suffrage. The other titles listed in the answer choices are too general.

9. **(3)** The passage states that the main difference between Keynes and traditional capitalists is that Keynes felt the government should be involved in the economy. This is stated in paragraph 2.

10. **(1)** You can infer that a "free economy" is an economy that doesn't have any government involvement. The answer to this item can be found in paragraph 2. The second sentence states that most capitalist economists felt the government should not get involved in the economy. The next sentence says that Keynes agreed with them that a free economy was the best.

11. **(3)** Lowered inflation is not mentioned as one of the benefits of public works projects. The other answer choices are mentioned in the third paragraph as benefits.

12. **(1)** It can be inferred that Keynes favored taxing and limiting imports because imports were bad for business. The fourth paragraph says that Keynes felt the government should tax and limit imports to protect businesses in the country.

13. **(3)** You can infer that climatologists are most interested in the earth's physical patterns. In the second paragraph, climate is listed as one of the physical patterns that geographers study. A climatologist is a person who studies climate.

14. **(1)** Answer choice 1 is an example of a biotic difference between Alaska and Florida. Biotic patterns are described in paragraph 2. Biotic patterns include the distribution of animals and plants. Only answer choice 1 deals with animals and plants.

15. **(1)** The main idea of the passage is that geographers look for patterns in the earth's surface. This is stated in the first and last paragraphs of the passage.

16. **(1)** The word "geosphere" most nearly means "earth." In the last paragraph, the word "geosphere" is mentioned. The word "earth" is used to explain what a geosphere is.

17. **(1)** An active crowd becomes a mob when there is tension. This statement is made at the beginning of paragraph 4.

18. **(4)** Of the four answer choices, the only one that is a fact is that sociologists separate crowds into two groups. The first three answer choices are all opinions that Amy Rand has about "John Doe" and crowd behavior.

19. **(3)** From the information in the passage, you can infer that one example of an expressive crowd is spectators watching a horse race. The second paragraph explains what an expressive crowd is. From this explanation, you can tell that answer choice 3 is a good example of an expressive crowd.

20. **(2)** Amy Rand would agree with the statement that people should not always be held responsible for their actions when they are in mobs. This statement is made in the last paragraph.

Part C: Science

1. **(1)** A change in a species' environment is the major reason that a species becomes extinct. You can find this information in paragraph 2.

2. **(3)** The word "extinct" most nearly means "die out." You can find this answer in the first sentence of the second paragraph.

3. **(2)** You can infer that many dinosaurs lived in swamps. The second paragraph tells you that changes in the earth's crust caused swamps to drain. This destroyed the habitat of many dinosaurs. You can infer that the dinosaurs lived in swamps.

4. **(4)** The dodo is used to show how a species can become extinct because of humans. The last paragraph tells you that sailors hunted dodos until they were extinct.

5. **(1)** The main purpose of the passage is to describe diabetes. The passage is about the cause, treatment, and effects of diabetes.

6. **(4)** Glucose is a sugar. You can find this information in the second paragraph.

7. **(3)** The statement that there are no treatments for diabetes is NOT supported by information in the passage. Paragraph 3 tells you that diabetes is treatable.

8. **(1)** A person who suffers from diabetes might be injected with insulin because his body is not producing enough insulin on its own. Paragraph 2 tells you that one form of diabetes occurs when the body doesn't produce enough insulin. Paragraph 3 tells you that a person suffering from a severe case of diabetes is injected with insulin. You can infer that a diabetic is injected with insulin because his body doesn't produce enough of it.

9. **(2)** The main idea of the passage is that elements are different from one another because they have different numbers of protons, neutrons, and electrons. You can find this information in the last paragraph of the passage.

10. **(4)** The statement that all elements are made up of the same basic particles is supported by the information in the passage. Paragraph 2 tells you that all atoms are made up of three basic particles. Paragraph 3 tells you that the main difference between the atoms of one element and the atoms of another element is the *number* of particles the atoms contain. You can infer that all elements are made up of the same three basic particles.

11. **(3)** From the diagram, you can infer that the symbol ⊖ stands for an electron. The first paragraph tells you that electrons are particles that circle around the atom's nucleus. You can infer that the particles circling the nucleus in the diagram are electrons.

12. **(3)** The nucleus of an atom contains protons and neutrons only. The first paragraph tells you that protons and neutrons make up the nucleus of an atom. The paragraph also tells you that electrons circle the nucleus. You can infer that protons and neutrons are the only particles that make up the nucleus.

13. **(4)** The main purpose of the passage is to explain light years. The passage defines a light year and explains how it is used.

14. **(4)** A ray of light can travel 6 trillion miles in one year. You can find this information in paragraph 3 of the passage.

15. **(1)** It would take a ray of light less than 2 seconds to travel from the earth to the moon. The first paragraph tells you that the moon is about 240,000 miles from earth. Paragraph 3 tells you that a ray of light travels at about 186,000 miles per second. In two seconds, a ray of light would travel twice as far — about 372,000 miles. You can infer that a ray of light could travel from the earth to the moon in less than two seconds.

16. **(2)** The statement that using light years makes it easier to measure great distances is supported by the passage. Paragraph 4 tells you that using light years as a measurement makes it easier to work with and understand distances.

ACKNOWLEDGMENTS

Page 30: From *Revenge of the Lawn* by Richard Brautigan. Copyright 1963, 1964, 1965, 1966, 1967, 1969, 1970, 1971 by Simon & Schuster.

Page 31: Copyright 1938, 1941, 1966, 1969 by Eudora Welty. Reprinted from "The Whistle" in her *A Curtain of Green and Other Stories* by permission of Harcourt Brace Jovanovich. Also being reprinted by permission of Russell & Volkening as agents for the author.

Page 32: "House Nigger," from *Tell Me How Long the Trains Been Gone* by James Baldwin. Copyright 1968 by James Baldwin. Reprinted by permission of Doubleday & Company.

Page 33: From "This Morning, This Evening, So Soon," in *Going to Meet the Man* by James Baldwin. Copyright 1948, 1951, 1957, 1958, 1960 by James Baldwin. A Dial Press Book; reprinted by permission of Doubleday & Company.

Page 34: From "The Harry Hastings Method" as it originally appeared in *Playboy* Magazine; copyright 1971 by Warner Law. Used by permission of Carol Russell Law.

Page 35: From *The Executioner's Song* by Norman Mailer. Copyright 1979 by Norman Mailer. Reprinted by permission of Little, Brown & Co.

Page 64: Reprinted by permission of Farrar, Straus and Giroux. Excerpt from "Parker's Back" in *The Complete Stories of Flannery O'Connor*. Copyright 1965, 1971 by the Estate of Mary Flannery O'Connor.

Page 65: Andrew A. Rooney. From "Fences" in *A Few Minutes with Andy Rooney*. Copyright 1981 by Essay Productions. Reprinted with the permission of Atheneum Publishers.

Page 66: From *Flowers for Algernon* by Daniel Keyes. Copyright 1959, 1966. Reprinted with the permission of Robert P. Mills.

Page 67: From "My Side of the Matter," in *A Tree of Night and Other Stories* by Truman Capote. Copyright 1945. Reprinted with the permission of Random House.

Page 71: From "Two Minutes on Vietnam" in *Malcolm X Speaks*. Copyright 1965 by Merit Publishers and Betty Shabazz. Reprinted with the permission of Pathfinder Press.

Page 108: From "The Stone Boy" by Gina Berriault. Copyright 1957. Reprinted with permission.

Page 109: From "Miss Brill" in *The Short Stories of Katherine Mansfield*. Copyright 1922, 1950. Reprinted with the permission of Alfred A. Knopf.